Animal Diaries
Life Cycles

A Butterfly's Life

by
Ellen Lawrence

Consultants:

Suzy Gazlay, MA
Recipient, Presidential Award for Excellence in Science Teaching

Susan Borkin, MS
Head of Life Sciences; Curator of Insects, Invertebrate
Zoology Department, Milwaukee Public Museum

Kimberly Brenneman, PhD
National Institute for Early Education Research, Rutgers University, New Brunswick, New Jersey

BEARPORT
PUBLISHING

New York, New York

Credits

Cover, © Cheryl E. Davis/Shutterstock; Cover L, © Ron Rowan Photography/Shutterstock; 3, © Arvind Balaraman/Shutterstock; 4TR, © Superstock; 4BR, © Michael Shake/Shutterstock; 5, © John A. Anderson; 6T, © Perry Correll/Shutterstock; 6B, © Larry West/FLPA; 7, © Wikipedia Creative Commons; 8, © Cathy Keifer/Shutterstock; 9T, © Cathy Keifer/Shutterstock; 9B, © Superstock; 10L, © Shutterstock; 10TR, © Cathy Keifer/Shutterstock; 10BR, © Cathy Keifer/Shutterstock; 11, © Andy Heyward/Shutterstock; 12, © Steven Russell Smith Photos/Shutterstock; 13, © Cathy Keifer/Shutterstock; 14, © Cathy Keifer/Shutterstock; 15TL, © Shutterstock/Andrew Park; 15TR, © Wikipedia Creative Commons; 15BL, © Chris Turner/Shutterstock; 15BR, © Ron Rowan Photography/Shutterstock; 17, © Doug Lemke/Shutterstock; 18, © Charles Shapiro/Shutterstock; 18–19, © Superstock; 20, © Lynn Hyman/Shutterstock; 21, © Cosmographics; 21TR, © Superstock; 22, © Shutterstock; 23TL, © Shutterstock; 23TC, © Shutterstock; 23TR, © Shutterstock; 23BL, © Superstock; 23BC, © Shutterstock; 23BR, © Doug Lemke/Shutterstock.

Publisher: Kenn Goin
Editorial Director: Adam Siegel
Creative Director: Spencer Brinker
Design: Emma Randall
Editor: Mark J. Sachner
Photo Researcher: Ruby Tuesday Books Ltd

Library of Congress Cataloging-in-Publication Data

Lawrence, Ellen, 1967-
  A butterfly's life / by Ellen Lawrence.
    p. cm. — (Animal diaries: Life cycles)
  Includes bibliographical references and index.
  ISBN-13: 978-1-61772-413-8 (library binding)
  ISBN-10: 1-61772-413-0 (library binding)
  1. Butterflies—Life cycles—Juvenile literature. I. Title.
  QL544.2.L39 2012
  595.78'9—dc23
                        2011043234

For more information, write to Bearport Publishing Company, Inc., 45 West 21st Street, Suite 3B, New York, New York 10010. Printed in the United States of America in North Mankato, Minnesota.

10 9 8 7 6 5 4 3 2 1

Contents

Name: **Sam**   Date: **July 31**

Fluttering Butterflies

Today, I saw two monarch butterflies in my backyard.

They were fluttering around each other.

Mom said they were a male and a female getting ready to **mate**.

After they've mated, the female butterfly will fly off and find a place to lay her eggs.

I hope she lays some in our yard!

Sam

The monarch butterfly in this picture is life-size. How big is it? Use a ruler to measure its wings.

legs

Butterflies are insects. Like all insects, they have six legs, three main body parts, and a hard covering called an exoskeleton.

Date: **August 1**

Hunting for Eggs

This morning I found a butterfly egg!

It was stuck underneath the leaf of a plant in our yard.

Mom told me monarch butterflies lay their tiny eggs under the leaves of milkweed plants.

I kept looking under milkweed leaves and found 50 eggs in our yard!

In real life, the eggs are the size of these white spots.

female laying eggs

a close-up photo of a monarch butterfly egg

6

milkweed leaf

After mating, a female monarch butterfly lays about 400 eggs. She lays one egg at a time.

egg

In spring and summer, try looking for butterfly eggs underneath leaves.

Date: **August 10**

Munch! Crunch!

After four days, tiny **caterpillars** began to hatch from the eggs!

They have long, wriggly bodies and eight pairs of legs.

The hungry little creatures quickly started munching on milkweed leaves.

I watch the caterpillars every day, and they never seem to stop eating.

They are growing bigger and bigger!

This is the size of the caterpillars when they hatch!

hatching caterpillar

egg

Go on a caterpillar hunt in your backyard or in a park. In a notebook, draw the different kinds of caterpillars you find. How are they alike? How are they different?

As a caterpillar grows bigger, its skin gets too tight. It squeezes out of its old skin, and there's a new one underneath.

old skin

new skin

head

10-day-old caterpillar

pairs of legs

9

Date: **August 18**

Wow! A Chrysalis

The caterpillars have been munching and growing for 14 days now.

Today, one of them hung upside down on a twig and began to wriggle.

Suddenly, the caterpillar's skin split open.

Under the skin I could see something shiny and green.

The caterpillar had changed into a **chrysalis**!

The chrysalis is inside a see-through case.

upside-down caterpillar

skin splitting open

chrysalis

life-size 14-day-old caterpillar

silk

chrysalis

Before it changes into a chrysalis, a caterpillar makes a pad of silk that it attaches to a leaf or twig. It hangs from the silk pad. The silk comes from inside the caterpillar's body.

11

A New Butterfly!

At first the chrysalis was green.

Now, I can see something orange and black moving around inside the chrysalis case.

Wow! The case just cracked open.

A beautiful orange and black monarch butterfly crawled out!

It took just ten days for the caterpillar to change into an adult butterfly.

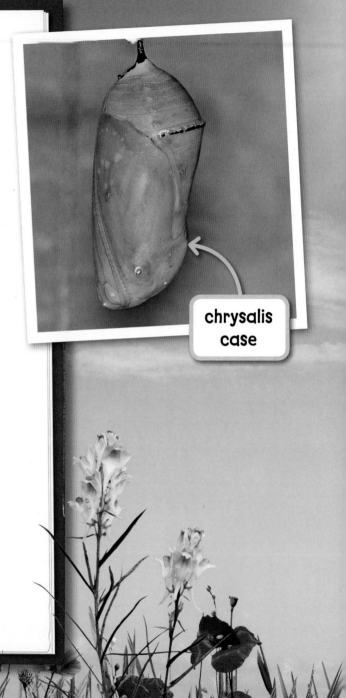

chrysalis case

chrysalis case

A butterfly's wings are crumpled and soft when it leaves its chrysalis case. It takes about 30 minutes for the wings to straighten out and harden. Then the butterfly can take off!

monarch butterfly

13

Amazing Changes

So many changes took place while the monarch was a chrysalis.

The insect's fat, striped body has become thin and black.

Now it has only six legs instead of sixteen.

The most amazing change is that it has grown wings.

When it was a caterpillar, the little insect could move around only by walking.

Now that it's an adult, it can fly from place to place!

All butterflies have the same life cycle. They hatch from an egg as a caterpillar. Then as a chrysalis, they change into an adult.

A Butterfly's Life Cycle

adult

egg

chrysalis

caterpillar

15

Butterfly Food

All the caterpillars have turned into adult butterflies now.

I watch them fly from flower to flower in the backyard.

They're looking for **nectar,** a sweet liquid that flowers make.

A butterfly sucks up nectar using a mouthpart called a **proboscis**.

A proboscis is a little like a drinking straw.

A caterpillar has mouthparts for crunching up solid food such as leaves. A butterfly drinks nectar or fruit juice using only its proboscis.

proboscis

Put slices of mushy orange, watermelon, or banana where butterflies are fluttering around. Watch them visit the fruit to drink the juices.

Date: **October 10**

A Great Trip South

It's fall, and I haven't seen any butterflies in the yard for a few days.

They have flown south to warm areas where they will spend the winter!

This journey is called a **migration**.

We live near Chicago, where it gets cold and snowy in winter.

If the butterflies stayed here, the cold weather would kill them.

The butterflies from my backyard will fly about 2,000 miles (3,219 km) to reach warm places!

In the fall, most monarch butterflies migrate to forests in Mexico or California. Once there, they crowd together on trees.

migrating butterflies

Date: **July 1**

They're Back!

Today, I saw monarchs in my backyard for the first time in nine months!

Mom told me that they aren't the same butterflies that left in October.

Those butterflies became too old and died on the journey back north.

They had young, however, that continued the journey.

These new butterflies also had young.

It's these butterflies that are in my yard today!

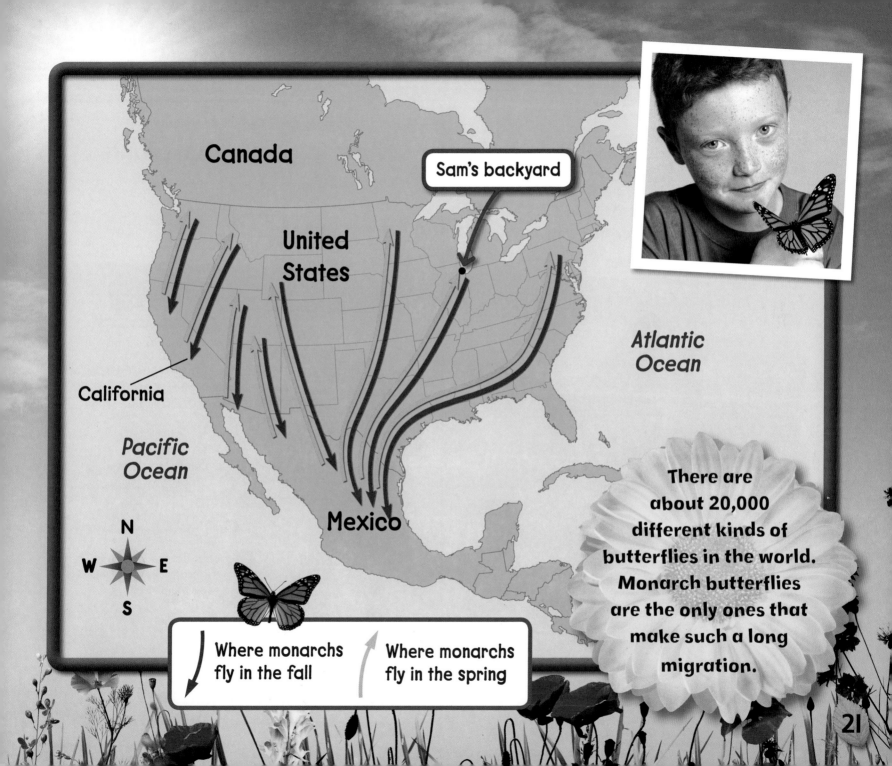

Canada

Sam's backyard

United States

California

Pacific Ocean

Atlantic Ocean

Mexico

N
W   E
S

Where monarchs fly in the fall   Where monarchs fly in the spring

There are about 20,000 different kinds of butterflies in the world. Monarch butterflies are the only ones that make such a long migration.

21

Science Lab

Help butterflies find nectar by planting seeds that will grow into flowers.

After the plants have grown, record in a diary what you see the butterflies doing around the flowers.

Garden Seeds
Verbena
A butterfly favorite!

Garden Seeds
Cosmos
A butterfly favorite!

Garden Seeds
Gaillardia
A butterfly favorite!

Garden Seeds
Milkweed
A butterfly favorite!

Science Words

caterpillars (KAT-ur-*pil*-urz) the young form of butterflies or moths

chrysalis (KRISS-uh-liss) the life stage of a butterfly between the caterpillar and adult; the chrysalis is inside a hard case

mate (MAYT) to come together in order to have young

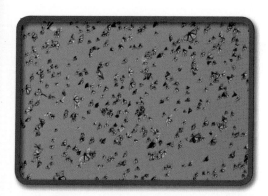

migration (mye-GRAY-shuhn) the movement of animals from one area to another, often when the seasons change

nectar (NEK-tur) a sweet liquid made by plants

proboscis (pruh-BOS-uhss) a long, tube-like nose or mouthpart used for feeding by some animals

Index

Read More

Frost, Helen, and Leonid Gore. *Monarch and Milkweed.* New York: Atheneum (2008).

Goldish, Meish. *Beautiful Butterflies (No Backbone!).* New York: Bearport (2008).

Sexton, Colleen. *The Life Cycle of a Butterfly.* Minneapolis, MN: Bellwether Media (2010).

Learn More Online

To learn more about monarch butterflies, visit **www.bearportpublishing.com/AnimalDiaries**

About the Author

Ellen Lawrence lives in the United Kingdom. Her favorite books to write are those about animals. In fact, the first book Ellen bought for herself, when she was six years old, was the story of a gorilla named Patty Cake that was born in New York's Central Park Zoo.

THE
WELL-KNIT
HOME

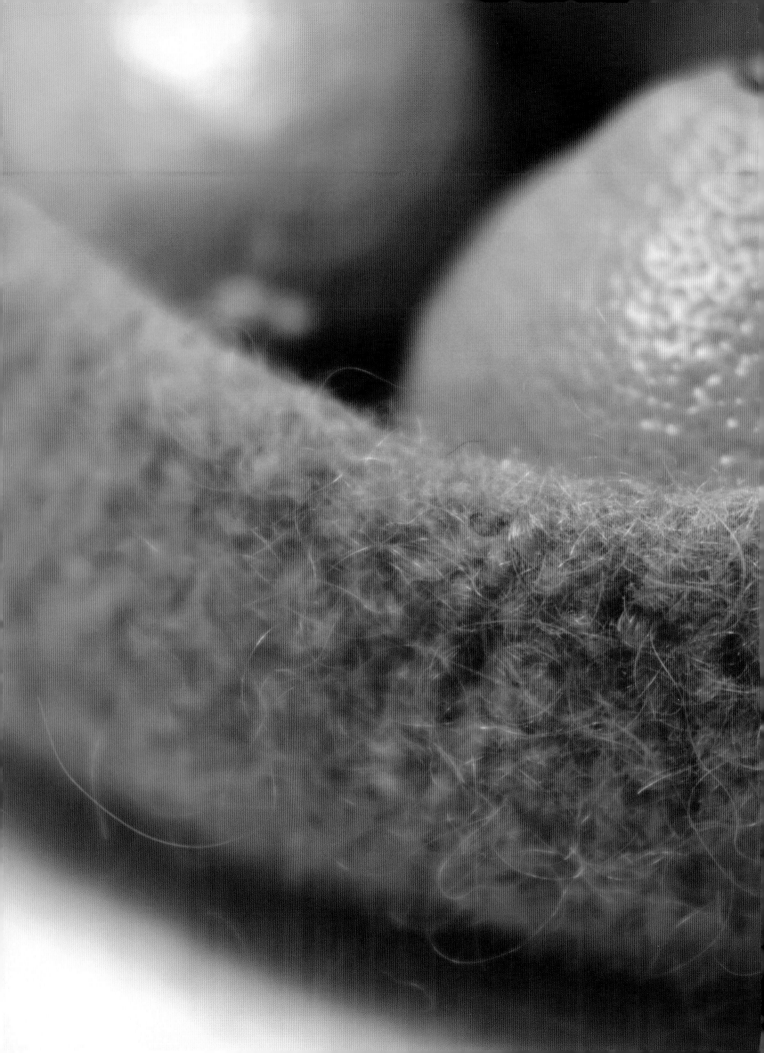

The Well-Knit Home

Gina Macris

Sterling Publishing Co., Inc.
New York

Library of Congress Cataloging-in-Publication Data

Macris, Gina.
 The well-knit home : simple techniques for beautiful results / Gina Macris.
   p. cm.
 Includes index.
 ISBN-13: 978-1-4027-3993-4
 ISBN-10: 1-4027-3993-1
 1. Knitting—Patterns. 2. House furnishings. I. Title.

TT825.M15495 2007
746.43'2043—dc22

                                        2006038784

10 9 8 7 6 5 4 3 2 1

Published by Sterling Publishing Co., Inc.
387 Park Avenue South, New York, NY 10016

Created by Lynn Bryan, The BookMaker
Design by Linda Wade
Photography by Amanda Hancocks
Pattern editor: Kate Buchanan

Distributed in Canada by Sterling Publishing
c/o Canadian Manda Group, 165 Dufferin Street,
Toronto, Ontario, Canada M6K 3H6

Distributed in the United Kingdom by
GMC Distribution Services,
Castle Place, 166 High Street, Lewes, East Sussex,
England BN7 1XU

Distributed in Australia by
Capricorn Link (Australia) Pty. Ltd.
P.O. Box 704, Windsor, NSW 2756, Australia

Sterling ISBN 10: 1-4027-3993-1
       ISBN 13: 978-1-4027-3993-4

For information about custom editions, special sales, premium and
corporate purchases, please contact Sterling Special Sales Department at
800-805-5489 or specialsales@sterlingpub.com.

CONTENTS

Living Knits 27

Dining Knits 48

Bedroom Knits 76

Baby Knits 104

Bath Knits 114

INTRODUCTION

Who says you can't transform a room with a few decorative pillows?

I remember my first house, a little jewel box that opened up on the inside to soaring ceilings, where I tried to make something new out of an amalgam of furniture from different places. I pulled together a loveseat and a sofa in an L-shaped seating area before the fireplace; two pieces unified with carefully made slipcovers in a soft brushed denim that promised to wear well. Then came a small Oriental rug, also heavy on the blues, and a glass coffee table that let the tones of the carpet shine through. Over time, other pieces were added, and art went up on the walls, but there was something about the living room seating area that was, well, blah—an expanse of blue, with more of the same underfoot.

A decorator friend told me to go out and get a bunch of pillows to break up all that blue. I was skeptical, but I figured I could return everything if the plan didn't work out. To guide my color selection, I looked carefully at the Oriental rug, where the deep blue background set off a range of hues that began with salmons and dusty pinks and ended with rusts and burgundies. Three trips to the store later, reflections of those colors had been elevated to the sofas, in clusters of brand new pillows that not only brightened the entire room, but pulled it all together in a way I hadn't thought possible.

One thing that exercise taught me was that accents make a room in the same way that accessories make an outfit. And as the projects of this book have emerged, I have started to look both at my knitting and at my home in a new light. I covet the little things that will make old spaces new. And my eyes have

been opened to the expanded possibilities of the knitted form, both in providing finishing details and in gestures of hospitality.

A deliciously soft throw is now an essential on a couch for visitors to wrap around them on a winter's day. Also, I can see myself sinking into the deep pile of a bath mat made from thick chenille cotton. I want always to have a washcloth going on the needles in an easy pattern, so that I can slip a couple of them into gift baskets filled with handmade soaps.

With textural accents being an important aspect of any interior, I have worked up patterns with an accent on stitches that produce texture in a knitted form. Hence the washcloths in a checked rib pattern, the owls in the baby blanket, and the fabulous pale green throw with a cable running through it.

For me, knitting is an adventure, sometimes pitching me into a forest, but eventually leading me to a clearing on the other side. The forest sometimes seems especially dense during the design process, with all the mathematical issues in which the numbers rule and I do not. Then, when I think I know all about a particular yarn, it tells me in no uncertain terms that there are some things it just won't do without special handling and respect. So I'm always learning—for the more I know, the easier the path through the woods.

As the projects for this book came together, I realized that accents for the home are a perfect starting point for your own designs. Any stitch pattern and any combination of color can be worked in a design for a pillow cover, a table runner, or a set of place mats. I can just hear everyone shudder over the prospect of doing the math involved in creating a design. But if you can swatch to get someone else's gauge, you can create your own gauge and make it work in your own design. With all these thoughts in mind, I'll try to guide you through the knitting forest in a primer on design in the first part of the book.

You will also learn about making bobbles for the project on page 82, and how to maneuver a double loop stitch, how to insert a zipper, and how to make a one-row buttonhole. I also talk about short rows, and crossing stitches for a two-tone placemat. Didn't I say knitting is an adventure? It's that and more. Knitting is a salve to the stresses of daily life. It has a way of slowing time to a manageable pace, allowing me to savor every moment while something wonderful grows out of my hands. I can easily imagine my knitting expanding to fill my days. Now wouldn't that be the ultimate luxury?

GINA MACRIS

KNIT
KNOWLEDGE

Learn about some of the stitches and techniques used in the projects: making bobbles, a one-row buttonhole, inserting a zipper, making loops, and basketweave stitch.

Designing with Yarn

Bringing shape and form to the projects in this book has evolved from one happy experiment after another, including various combinations of stitch patterns, color, and texture in fibers as different as hemp and alpaca. This short design essay takes you through some of the mental exercises that led to the final projects in the hope that you, too, may gain the confidence to go where the yarn spins you.

In thinking about accents for the home, I was eager to reach beyond the conventional in the yarns and stitches associated with knitted items, although there's always a place in my heart for cabling, with all its varied richness.

The design journey began when my eye fixed on a fiber that evoked images of rooms filled with light and the clean lines of modern furniture. There was a crisp, fresh quality about the way the dye took to the fiber. It was definitely made from plant material but was unlike any cotton I'd ever seen in a yarn store. I discovered it was hemp. I bought two skeins, one in pearly white, the other in a light gray and took them home with me and waited for inspiration.

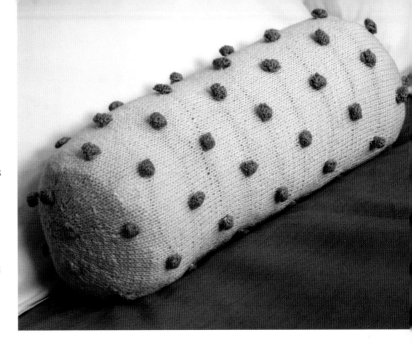

The yarn is usually the starting point in a knitted design. Unlike an interior designer or clothing designer who buys fabric, the knitwear designer creates her own, and it is the yarn that inevitably places parameters on the type of fabric that will emerge.

Other elements of design—including color, texture, overall line, proportion, and function—are intertwined with the choice of yarn or yarns, as well as the stitch patterns that will best show them off. There are endless stitch-and-color combinations and finding the right one for a specific project is half the fun of the design process.

Samples, or swatches, of various stitches and color combinations are essential design tools. It's worth keeping these unique pieces and cataloguing them, along with their instructions, because swatching helps deepen a knitter's understanding of the different ways in which a specific yarn can be manipulated.

Knitters today benefit from centuries of inventiveness that has been passed down, much of it recorded in stitch dictionaries published over decades. The most exhaustive collection is the work of Barbara G. Walker. With the hemp in mind, I turned to one of her books. The stiffness of the hemp spoke to me of a combination that would contrast texture as well as color. I settled on a short-row pattern that juxtaposed bunches of purl stitches against a stockinette background. A pillow cover would be the best canvas for showing off the stitch pattern.

The longer I looked at the swatch I had made, the more the bunches of purl stitches wanted to come off the surface of the pillow entirely and become bobbles. Thus was born the idea for a second pillow cover in hemp, a stockinette tube covered in bobbles. Where the gray had dominated in the first one, white became the main color in the second pillow cover, with bobble accents in grey, all designed to fit around a bolster.

As you can see, working with yarn is a creative process, one that can take you far away from a starting point. There have been many times when I have declared I am finished with a design, only to look at it again a few days later and see it in a new light. That reaction generally demands I make yet another swatch.

Above
Rows of bobbles in a contrasting color adorn a cover for a bolster pillow. The piece is worked back and forth, end to end, with a bobble-button closure

Opposite above
Delicate yarns can be paired with a stronger yarn to make an impact

Opposite below
Varying thicknesses of yarn make a tempting trio.

Most projects go through several versions before I find I am no longer compelled to look at them after making what I consider the final changes.

The melon and white baby blanket evolved this way. It started with a seed stitch border in melon. Then the second color came on board. But how to arrange the two colors? Where was the whimsy? (A baby blanket should be sweet and whimsical, don't you agree?) I recalled an owl pattern made of cables and so I began to construct owls, one on top of the other. As I worked, the owls got bigger and fatter along with the cables. Then I figured out how to tuck in a couple of bobbles for eyes beneath the sweep of the owl's brow. Finally, a patch of seed stitch on the breast picked up the seed stitch from the blanket border. To my delight, the seed stitch insert had a way of puffing up the shape of Mr. Owl even more than if I had left him cabled entirely in stockinette stitch. At this point I thought I was almost done.

TIP

The critical element in arriving at the gauge is the size of the knitting needle. When instructions specify a needle size, it is a starting point in any knitter's attempts to match the designer's number of stitches and rows per inch (cm), but it is by no means an ironclad dictum.

Too small a sample calls for a larger needle; too large a swatch means a smaller needle is required. It goes without saying that duplicating the gauge in pattern instructions is prerequisite to starting the project.

Above
The wise owl pattern is created using a cable pattern with bobbles to act as its eyes. Each owl sits in a sea of white stockinette stitch, creating a bigger picture.

But I was wrong. I had planned to arrange the owls in a melon-and-white checkerboard and started to work on larger swatches that combined the two colors. However, the checkerboard design was not to be. The owl squares would not juxtapose themselves neatly with plain stockinette squares of the same size. The numbers just didn't work, threatening to scuttle the entire project, but I would not let go of those owls. I kept looking at swatches and calculations, hoping for a miracle, but then it dawned on me that the owls should float on a white background.

One of the things I love about knitting is that there is always a new way to look at creating a knitted design, ranging from the strong vertical lines in the mock-cabled throw on page 28, to the exuberance of the Carmen Miranda ruffles in the black and white tea cozy, page 56. I also love the symmetry of the chevron pattern in the silk table runner on page 52 and seen below, which creates peaks and valleys in a dramatic black and white expanse of cloth.

Designing with yarn is about confidence with experimentation, plus the use of color and texture to achieve the look you desire. The more experimental work I do, the more I'm certain that I've only skimmed the surface of possibilities. I hope you find the same pleasure in exploring new ways with yarn and stitches, and that the designs on the pages in this book offer an insight into design.

THE MATH

The numbers can either be a barrier, or they can be your friends, enabling you to create new designs or adapt existing ones. Knitting math is rooted in gauge: the ratio, or proportion, of stitches and rows in samples of one or more square inches (cm).

To work up the numbers for a specific size, knit a swatch 4" (10cm) square. Let's say 20 stitches and 28 rows. Divide the number of stitches by the width of the swatch to get the number of stitches per inch (cm). Here, 20 stitches divided by 4" (10cm) is 5 stitches per inch (per cm). If you want to make a pillow cover 12" (30cm) wide with the gauge described above, multiply 5 stitches per inch (per cm) by 12. The total number of stitches to be cast on is 60.

To get the row gauge, divide the total number of rows in the swatch by the length. Multiply the number of rows per inch (cm) by the desired length. In the example, 28 rows divided by 4 gives a count of 7 rows to the inch (cm).

Above
The use of plain black and white is an effective design tool when you use the two to contrast with each other.

Right
More black and white but this time it is the chevron stitch that creates the interest, along with the silken yarn

SKILLS TO KNOW

A few of the techniques used in some of the projects in this book warrant special attention. Expand your skills by delving into the following step-by-step instructions for the several valuable techniques that add versatility to your knitting skills. What might look difficult is often as easy as 1, 2, 3 when you learn how.

Inserting a zipper, for example, into either a pillow cover or a hot water bottle makes it easier to remove the cover and clean it when necessary. Similarly, learning how to make a simple thing such as a sturdy buttonhole that will keep its shape over time in the fabric of a pillow cover is essential. Also consider the advantages of being able to create a basketweave effect using crossed stitches without having to pick up and put down a cable needle each time. You will become a veritable speed demon on the needles. Working with

chenille can be a challenge so there is advice on how to make this easier. The loops on the pillow on page 36 are made with chenille yarn so some step-by-step instructions for making loops are included in this section of the book.

Finally, my thoughts on making bobbles, beautiful bobbles. I am passing on my know-how in an attempt to ease you into the art of creating deliberate bumps all over your knitting. They look fabulous, and really are easy to make.

Above
The loopy front of the cushion contrasts with the seed stitch used on the back of the cover.

Left
A contrast in stitches creates an interesting textural surface on this this pale blue throw.

Right
The final placemat has a dense basketweave pattern.

BASKETWEAVE STITCH

You can cross stitches without a cable needle. The illustrations show the methods for crossing stitches on right-side rows, 1 and 3. Full pattern instructions for the placemat are on Page 68.

Row 1

1. With B, k2, *tug first st on left needle to elongate it.

2. Drop st in front of work, and k2. Tug the st dropped in front so it does not disappear while you are knitting the next two loops.

3. Pick up dropped st. Transfer it to right needle without working it. Rep from *, ending k1.

Row 3

On Row 3, hold the right needle absolutely still during the second and third steps.

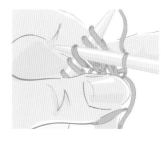

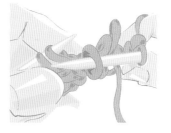

1. With yarn A, k1, *pass right needle in front of work and insert it purlwise in front of third st on left needle.

2. Withdraw left needle from first three sts, dropping the first two and leaving third on the right needle in front of work.

3. Move left needle behind right needle and pick up the two dropped sts.

4. Do not work st which has crossed to right needle. K2, rep from * ending k2.

KNIT WITH CHENILLE

Chenille yarn has a wonderful luster and a plush surface but needs special handling to look its best. To work better with, rather than against, the yarn, it is important to understand how this yarn is made.

It is produced using a central strand made up of very tightly wound, long fibers. Shorter, softer fibers (the pile) are then spun into these center strands to give the yarn the appearance of a very thin woven fabric. The long, sturdy center strand gives the yarn its durability, and the short fibers gives it the softness. The pile makes a nap that reflects light differently, depending on the direction from which it is viewed. Chenille may be made of cotton, rayon, acrylic, polypropylene, or even silk fibers.

Chenille yarn requires a firm hand to keep it under control and counteract its tendency to worm (spring little twisted tails) in the middle of the work. If there are spaces between your stitches, go down a needle size (two, if necessary) to tighten up the fabric. Sometimes you may have to work on the tips of the needles to get densely formed stitches while avoiding too much stress on the yarn. Chenille has absolutely no elasticity.

When it is subjected to excessive strain, it will break. If a break does occur occasionally, treat the problem as if you were starting a new ball of yarn, weaving the old and new tails into the fabric you have already knitted.

Whether the yarn cooperates, or fights, with you also depends on the type of needles you use and how you deal with the nap. I've found that wooden needles let chenille slide more easily than some other surfaces, but experiment yourself and draw your own conclusions. To help the chenille glide over your needles, it is important to work with the smooth side of the nap flowing away from your knitting. The cotton chenille yarn recommended for two of the projects in this book comes in cones wound with the smooth side already wrapped in the correct direction.

But if you should be working with a ball of yarn, it is wise to check the nap before beginning to knit. Search out both ends of the yarn and run your fingers along them. Start knitting with the end that feels smoother as you move your hand away from your body, back toward the ball. Working against the nap will add unneeded stress to the yarn.

The lack of elasticity makes chenille yarn a poor choice to use for sewing together pieces of a project. Instead, use a plain cotton yarn or cotton and synthetic blend for seaming.

The pattern stitches for the chenille projects have been chosen to minimize the tendency of chenille to bias, or slant, to the left or right as it is worked. If biasing does occur, use smaller needles, or use matching sewing thread as a companion to the chenille to stabilize the fabric while you knit. Above all, take the time to experiment with the yarn before launching into your knitted project.

Above
The front of the cushion, with its loop stitch, contrasts with the plainer stitch used on the back of the cover.

Opposite
The loops look fantastic when you seen them close up.

DOUBLE LOOP STITCH

Double loop stitch makes a thick shag pile that works as an accent or the main event. If you want to imitate fur, just cut the loops open when the knitting is completed and trim them to a uniform length.

In forming the double loops, hold your left thumb far enough away from your work so that it does not get in the way of the action on the needles, and can provide a stable anchor for the loops in progress. Do not worry that the loops might not be all the exact same length. Small variations will not be noticeable. With practice, you will soon hit your stride with this style of knitting and the loops will become a uniform size without you even noticing!

1. Knit one stitch, keeping old loop on left needle.

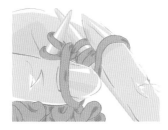

2. Bring yarn forward between needles and wrap over thumb, as shown.

3. Wind yarn to the back and over tip of left needle. Bring yarn forward.

4. Return yarn to the back of work between the two needles.

5. Knit both loops on left needle.

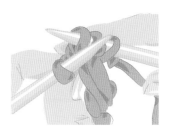

6. Pass second stitch on right needle over first stitch and tug at double loops to tighten.

INSTALLING A ZIPPER

Installing a zipper need not be intimidating, even if you think you know nothing about sewing. All it takes is patience. Here are step-by-step instructions.

1. Pick up stitches along the length of the piece where the zipper will be installed, and work a couple of rows of garter or seed stitch for the selvage. Bind off.

2. Work a row of single crochet to make a seam allowance to fill the gap.

3. Put the zipper face down on the wrong side, aligning the teeth along the edges that are basted together. Pin, or baste with sewing thread, the zipper in place.

4. Turn project to the right side and remove the yarn basting from the selvages. Unzip the zipper and sew, by hand or machine, along the outside of the zipper teeth. If sewing by hand, work from the front, using a back stitch in a matching thread.

Prepare the placket

Because the knitted edges must lie flat, they need a cooperative selvage, such as two rows of garter stitch or seed stitch . If the selvage is not part of the pattern, you can make one (*see Illustration 1*). Skip an opening every two or three stitches so the edges do not curl.

In the pillow covers in this book, the zipper runs along most of one side, stopping short of the corners. This short-stop, requires compensation for the fact there is no seam allowance above and below the zipper. You can close the opening by stitching edge to edge between the two knitted pieces, above and below the zipper. Or you can add a row of single crochet (*see Illustration 2*).

To ensure the edges are aligned and the zipper teeth do not show through to the front, baste the selvages together (*see Illustration 3*). Finally, sew the zipper to the matching edges (*see Illustration 4*). To finish, on the wrong side, whip stitch the edges of the zipper tape to knitted fabric to secure it.

ONE-ROW BUTTONHOLE

The one-row buttonhole looks good, needs no finishing, and holds up under heavy wear. It calls for multiple maneuvers over a small number of stitches, but once it's done, it's done. You don't have to return to the buttonhole in subsequent rows.

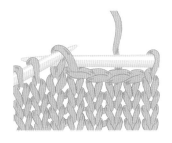  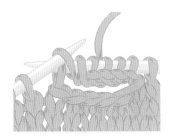

1. When in position for the buttonhole, bring the yarn to the front and slip a stitch purlwise. Pass the yarn to the back and leave it there. *Move first stitch from left needle to right needle. Pass second stitch on right needle over the first, binding off one. Repeat from * three times more. Move first stitch on right needle to left needle. Turn work.

2. Using cable cast-on, cast on five stitches in the following method: *Insert right needle between first and second stitches on left needle. Make a loop, draw it forward and place it on the left needle. Repeat from * four times more. Turn work.

3. With yarn in back, slip first stitch on left needle to right needle. Pass second stitch on right needle over first stitch to complete buttonhole. Work to end of row.

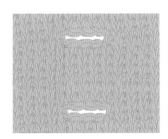

4. Two completed buttonholes sit neatly within the body of the knitting.

MAKING BOBBLES

Knitters don't always love making bobbles, but they love the way bobbles enrich their knitting. Bobbles come in many sizes. Here are instructions for a version of the four-stitch bobble, one of the most common. So now it is a case of learn to love your bobbles!

I used to be intimidated by the idea of making bobbles until I spent a summer vacation on the beach, knitting them, day in and day out, for a sweater I just had to have. After finishing two two–tiered bobble borders and a field of bobble flowers that literally covered the front and back of this cardigan, I was no longer cowed by these little protuberances.

The experience was one of my earliest lessons in muscling yarn to do what I want. Remember, knitters, you are the boss.

Bobbles can be made in various styles and sizes. For the owl blanket on page 106, the bobbles had to be small, so as to not overpower the other elements of the design. But the bolster pillow on page 82 called for substantial bobbles to serve as buttons for the closure. Because I wanted the bobbles on the pillow to pop out of the background, I went for the maximum contrast, both in texture and color. They are worked in reverse stockinette stitch in grey against a stockinette stitch background in pearly white.

Each bobble begins with a single stitch that is expanded to a cluster of up to six stitches. There are literally dozens of variations on the construction of the bobble. Usually, one or more rows of the bobble stitches are worked, turning back and forth in mid-row, before the bobble cluster is reduced to one stitch again and you move along in the work.

Bobbles can grow out of the knitting in hand or can be worked separately and sewn in after the fact. As with anything else in knitting, opinions differ on the best approach. Working bobbles in place definitely slows down the knitting, but attaching bobbles to a project upon its completion can also be a chore. It's up

to you, but keep in mind that if you choose a method that differs from a particular pattern, it may affect the gauge. For example, the bobbles knitted into the bolster pillow made for a looser gauge than the gauge usually associated with a plain stockinette background.

There is more than one way to grow the cluster of stitches needed for a bobble. The easiest method incorporates yarn-overs. These are usually three or five-stitch bobbles, with the yarn-overs accounting for the second and fourth stitches. Another method creates all the needed stitches by knitting into the back and front of the starter stitch. And yet a third alternates knit and purl stitches. It is important to work as tightly as possible to counteract the tendency that bobbles have of leaving some space between stitches. As long as the total number of stitches is not changed, one approach to all these increases may be substituted for another. The yarn-over method may even be used for the six-stitch bobble in the bolster pillow. (In the starter stitch, k1, yo, k1, yo, k1, p1.) No one will ever know that the yarn-overs are not symmetrical.

I am guilty of manhandling the yarn to get what I want. I pull on the starter stitch to widen it up a bit. I work on the tips of the needles to cram in as many stitches as necessary for the bobble. Once each new loop is formed, I gently push it onto the shaft of the right needle, elongating the loop as I go. When the bobble is completed and down to one stitch, I pull on the bobble to pop it into position on the right side of the work. I then tug on the working yarn, and knit the next stitch in the pattern as closely as possible, so as to minimize the space between the two stitches. You will find this easier the more you attempt the stitch.

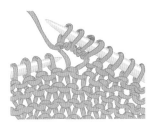

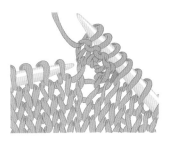

1. On the right side, work to the anchor, or starter, stitch for the bobble. In that stitch k1, p1, k1, p1 for four stitches. Drop the original loop off the left needle, leaving the four new stitches on the right needle.

2. Turn the work. Purl the four bobble stitches and turn the work again. Knit these four bobble stitches in the second row. Turn the work. Purl the same four stitches. You have now completed three rows in reverse stockinette stitch over the bobble stitches, without working the overall pattern.

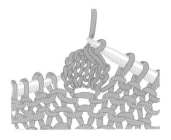

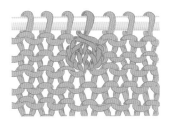

3. Turn the work to the right side. Slip the first two stitches, moving them across to the right needle. Knit the next two stitches together, then pass the first two stitches, one by one, over the first loop on the left needle.

4. With the finished bobble reduced to one stitch, continue working across the right side of your work in the pattern that has been established.

TIP

If you have difficulty fitting multiple increases in a single stitch, try tugging at the starter stitch to elongate it. Knit tightly, working on the tips of the needles and using as little of the starter stitch as possible while each increase is made. Then gradually elongate each new loop as you move it onto the shaft of the right needle. Your patience and determination will be rewarded.

THE PROJECTS

LIVING KNITS

In this chapter, you will find something for the living spaces in your home, or even for a friend's new home. The projects include elegant throws, pillow covers made of hemp, and one with loops, plus a felted bowl and a vase cover.

An Elegant Throw

Envelop yourself in a luxuriously soft oversized throw, the perfect accessory for your sofa or chaise. Mock cables with eyelets run the length of the piece, adding an airy feeling without sacrificing warmth.

Skill Level: ◖■■■◗

Materials

Yarn:	Rowan Classic Yarns Cashsoft DK 142yd (130m)/1.75oz (50g) ball
Color:	509 Lime
Amount:	18 balls
Total Yardage:	2,556yd (2340m)
Needles:	US 9 (5.5mm) or size to get gauge
Gauge:	Approx. 20 sts and 26 rows = 4" (10cm) in mock cable
Finished size:	Approx. 48" x 53" (122 cm by 135 cm)

INSTRUCTIONS

Cast on 239 sts.
Row 1: Sl 1 purlwise, knit to end.
Rows 2-10: Repeat Row 1.

Begin pattern
Row 1: Sl 1 purlwise, k6, *p4, k2 tog, k1, yo, p1, yo, k1, ssk, p6, ssk, k1, yo, k5, yo, k1, k2tog, p2; rep from * 6 times more, p4, k2tog, k1, yo, p1, yo, k1, ssk, p4, k7.

Row 2: Sl 1 purlwise, k 6, *k4, p2, k3, p2, k6, yo, p11, yo, k2; rep from * 6 times more, k4, p2, k3, p2, k4, k7.

Row 3: Sl 1 purlwise, k 6, *p3, k2tog, k1, yo, p3, yo, k1, ssk, p5, p1 tbl, yo, sl 1, ssk, psso, k2tog (k1, p1, k1 in next st), sl 1, ssk, psso, k2tog, yo, p1 tbl, p2; rep from* 6 times more, p3, k2tog, k1, yo, p3, yo, k1, ssk, p3, k7.

Row 4: Sl 1 purlwise, k 6, *k3, p2, k5, p2, k6, k1 tbl, p3, k1, p3, k1 tbl, k3; rep from * 6 times more, k3, p2, k5, p2, k3, k7.

Row 5: Sl 1 purlwise, k 6, *p2, k2tog, k1, yo, p1, k3, p1, yo, k1, ssk, p6, k2tog, k1, yo, p1, yo, k1, ssk, p4; rep from * 6 times more, p2, k2tog, k1, yo, p1, k3, p1, yo, k1, ssk, p2, k7.

Row 6: Sl 1 purlwise, k6, *k2, p2, k2, p3, k2, p2, k6, p2, k3, p2, k4; rep from * 6 times more, k2, p2, k2, p3, k2, p2, k2, k7.

Row 7: Sl 1 purlwise, k 6, *p2, ssk, k1, yo, k5, yo, k1, k2tog, p5, k2tog, k1, yo, p3, yo, k1, ssk, p3; repeat from * 6 times more, p2, ssk, k1, yo,

Above
The details of the design from the back (left) and the front (right). The arch of the mock cable, enhanced by eyelets, is set against a background of reverse stockinette stitch.

k5, yo, k1, k2tog, p2, k7.
Row 8: Sl 1 purlwise, k6, * k2, yo, p11, yo, k5, p2, k5, p2, k3, repeat from * 6 times more, k2, yo, p11, yo, k2, k7.

Row 9: Sl 1 purlwise, k 6, *p2, p 1 tbl, yo, sl 1, ssk, psso, k2tog (k1,p1,k1 in next st), sl 1, ssk, psso, k2tog, yo, p1 tbl, p4, k2tog, k1, yo, p1, k3, p1, yo, k1, ssk, p2; repeat from * 6 times more, p2, p1 tbl, yo, sl1, ssk, psso, k2tog (k1, p1, k1 in

next st), sl 1, ssk, psso, k2tog, yo, p1 tbl, p2, k7.
Row 10: Sl 1 purlwise, * k3, k 1tbl, p3, k1, p3, k1 tbl, k5, p2, k2, p3, k2, p2, k2, rep from * 6 times more, k3, k 1tbl, p3, k1, p3, k1 tbl, k3, k7.

Repeat 10 rows of pattern until throw measures approx 51¾" (131.5cm), ending with a WS row.
Work 10 rows garter st.
Bind off.

Mock Cable Pattern Chart

The color section signifies it is the final segment in the row and is knit once only.

To Use Chart
Right-side rows: Slip first st of each row purlwise, k next 6 sts *(not shown on chart)*, repeat the white section of the chart (sts 1 to 34) 7 times and repeat the green section of the design once. K next 7 sts *(not shown on chart)*.

Wrong-side rows: Slip first st of each row purlwise, k next 6 sts *(not shown on chart)*. Proceed with green pattern repeat once, then repeat the white section of the chart (34 to 1) 7 times. K next 7 sts *(not shown on chart)*.

I	K on right side, p on wrong side
—	P on right side, k on wrong side
⅄	K2tog
人	SSK
A	K through back loop
O	Yarn over
⅄	Sl 1 st, k2tog, psso
❤	K1, p1, k1 in next st
■	No st

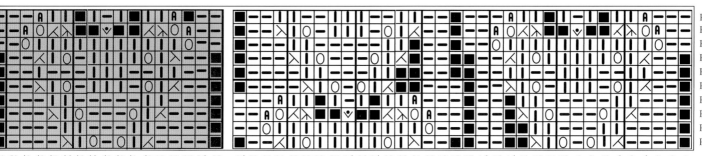

A Heavenly
Hemp Cover

Hemp lends crisp definition to changes in texture and color in this contemporary pillow cover. The design statement is made using short rows. The hemp softens with washing.

Skill Level: ▰▰▰▱

Materials

Yarn:	ALLHEMP 6 150yd (137m)/3.2oz (90g)
Color:	For MC, Classic Hemp For CC, Pearl
Amount:	3 balls MC, 1 ball CC
Total Yardage:	450yd (411m) for MC, 150yd (137m) for CC
Needles:	US 5 (3.75mm) or size to get gauge
Gauge:	For front: 18.5 sts and 33 rows = 4" (10cm) in pattern stitch For back: 20 sts and 32 rows = 4" (10cm) in stockinette stitch
Finished Size:	Approx 18" (45.7cm) x 18" (45.7cm)

Notes:

* It will be easier to get gauge if the hemp is washed before it is used. To prevent tangles, insert skeins in an old pair of panty hose before putting them in the washer. Air dry.

* Cast-on includes 2 selvage stitches that are knit on RS rows and purled on WS rows throughout. They are not incorporated in pattern directions that follow.

INSTRUCTIONS

Pillow front:

With MC, cast on 86 sts.
To create selvage for zipper, knit 2 rows

Begin pattern:

Rows 1 and 3: (WS): With MC, purl.

Row 2: With CC, knit.

Row 4: With CC, k11, *turn; sl1 wyif, k3, turn; p4, k12; repeat from* ending k1.

Row 5: With CC, k5, *turn; p4, turn; k3, sl1 wyib, k12; rep from * ending k7.

Row 6: With MC, k8, *sl 2 wyib, k10; repeat from * ending k2.

Rows 7, 8, and 9: With MC, repeat rows 1, 2, and 3.

Row 10: With CC, k5, *turn; sl 1 wyif, k3, turn; p4, k12; repeat from * ending k7.

Row 11: With CC, k11, *turn; p4, turn; k3, sl 1 wyib, k12; rep from * ending k1.

Row 12: With MC, k2, *sl 2 wyib, k10; rep from * ending k8.

Repeat pattern over 84 sts until piece measures 18" (45.7cm) in length.
Bind off all sts.

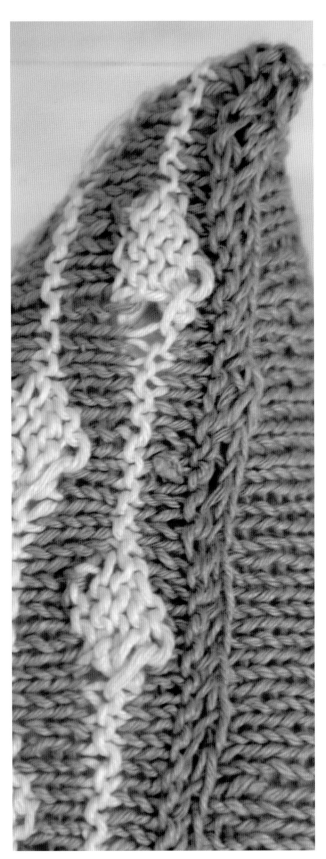

Opposite page
Short rows of purl bumps in white, set
against a background of grey stockinette
stitch, make an arresting pattern, seen in
detail, left, and above.

Pillow back:
Cast on 101 sts.

To create a selvage for a zipper, knit two rows.

Maintaining a knit selvage on each side of work
as for the front, work in St st. until piece
measures 18" (45.7cm) in length. Bind off all sts.

Finishing:
Block the pillow back and front

Install the zipper according to the directions on
page 22. Use a matching thread to seam the
pillow on the three remaining sides.

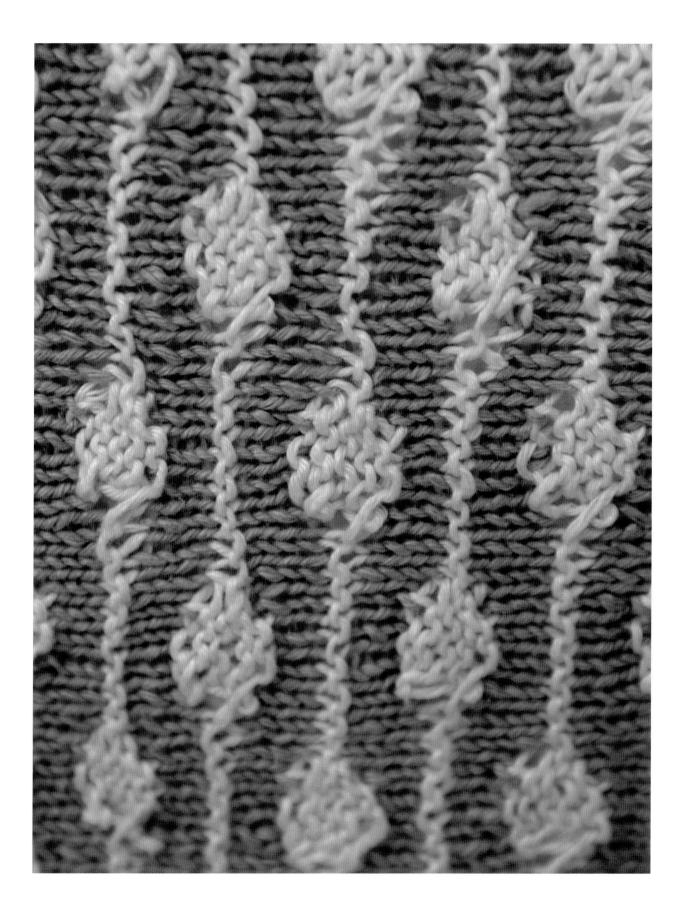

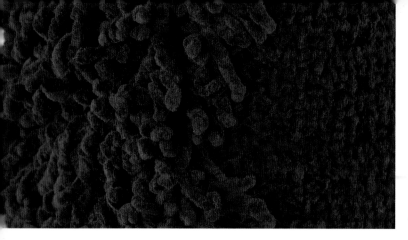

Shag is used along with double loop stitch in this accent pillow cover. Its deep pile spells funky fun on a sofa or a single chair.

Skill Level: ◼◼◼◻
Materials

Yarn: Halcyon Yarn Casco Bay Bulky Chenille 550yd (503m)/llb (454g) cone
Color: 201 Brown
Amount: 1 cone for small pillow, 2 cones for large pillow cover
Total Yardage: 550yd (503m) for small pillow cover, 1100yd (1006m) for large pillow cover
Needles: US 10 (6mm) or size to get gauge
US 8 (5mm) or size to get gauge
Gauge: For pillow front, 11.2 sts and 17 rows =4" (10cm) in pattern stitch before washing and drying and 10.5 sts and 19 rows =4" (10cm) after washing and drying, using larger needles
For pillow back, 14 sts and 25 rows = 4" (10cm) in pattern stitch before washing and drying and 13.5 sts and 27.5 rows = 4" (10cm) after washing and drying, using smaller needles
Finished Size: Small: 12" x 12" (30cm x 30cm); Large: 18" (45cm) x 18" (45cm)

Details of how to knit a double loop stitch are on page 21. Refer to these illustrations for guidance.

Front:
With larger needles, cast on 34 (50)sts.
Row 1: (WS): Purl.
Row 2: K1 selvage st.
Begin double loop stitch: *Knit 1 st, leaving old loop on left needle, bring working yarn forward between the two needles, pass it around the left thumb from top to bottom and to the back again. Wrap the yarn again, this time over the left needle, around the thumb and to the back of the work. Insert right needle knitwise in both loops on the left needle and knit one stitch. Pass first stitch on right needle over stitch just knit. Tug the loops to tighten. Rep from * until 1 st remains, k1.

Repeat rows 1 and 2 until pillow front is 12" (30cm) or (18") (45cm) long, depending on which size you are knitting. Bind off.

Back: With smaller needles, cast on 42 (64)sts.
Row 1: *K1, p1, rep from * to end.
Row 2: *P1, k1, rep from * to end.

Repeat these two rows until piece measures 12" (18)" [(30cm (45cm)]. Bind off.

Finishing:
Wash and dry the pieces of the completed pillow cover. Install a zipper on one side of the cover, following the instructions on page 22. Using plain cotton yarn that matches the color of the chenille, sew together the three remaining sides.

Above
The textures of the front and back of the shaggy chenille cushion cover are a study in contrast

Opposite
A thicket of double loop stitch makes an interesting accent on a pillow cover for a chair or sofa.

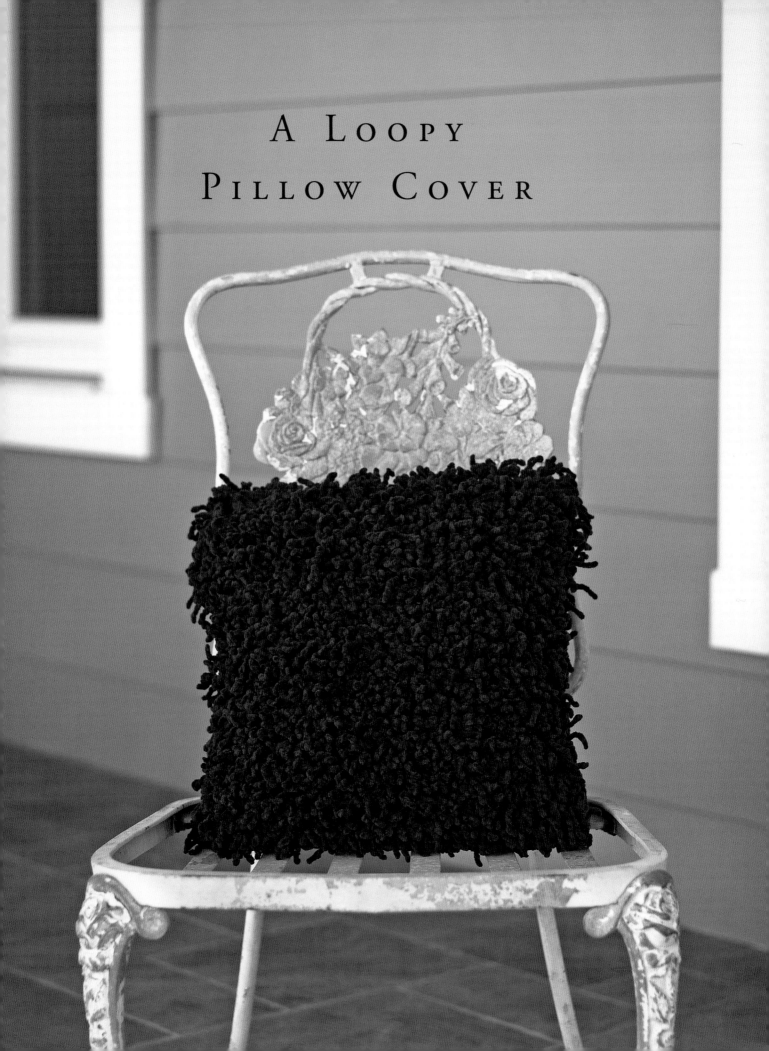

A Loopy
Pillow Cover

A TEXTURED BOWL

Sturdy felting makes a squared-off bowl that will add cachet to a desktop or end table. It makes a fashion statement all by itself.

Skill Level:	■□□
Materials	
Yarn:	Lamb's Pride worsted 190yd (173m)/4oz (113g)
Color:	M-04, Charcoal Heather
Amount:	1 skein
Total Yardage:	190yd (173m)
Needles:	One set US 15 (10mm) double-pointed needles, or size to get gauge
	1 crochet hook US N (10mm) or size to match needles
Gauge:	Before felting, approx. 10 sts and 12 rows = 4" (10cm)
	After felting, 12½ sts and 18½ rows = 4" (10cm)
Finished Size:	Approx. 3" (7.6cm) in diameter and 2½" (6.3cm) tall

Note: Two strands of yarn are used together throughout the pattern.

INSTRUCTIONS

Using a crochet hook and two strands of yarn, chain 4 sts. Pull the loop through the first chain to form a ring. Place the loop on a knitting needle and pick up 3 additional sts around the ring. (4 sts)

Round 1: Inc. 1 st in each st. (8 sts)
Round 2: Knit even.

Round 3: * Inc. 1, k1, rep from * to end. (16 sts)
Round 4: Knit even.
Round 5: *K1, inc. 1, k3, inc. 1, rep from * to end. (24 sts)
Round 6: Knit even.
Round 7: *K1, inc.1, k5, inc. 1, repeat from * to end. (32 sts)
Round 8: Knit even.
Round 9: *K1, inc.1, k7, inc.1, rep from * to end. (40 sts)
Round 10: Knit even.
Round 11: *K1, inc.1, k9, inc.1, rep from * to end. (48 sts)

Knit 10 rounds even.

Next round: *K1, k2 tog, k9, ssk, repeat from * to end. (40 sts)
Next round: Knit even.
Next round: K1, k2 tog, k7, ssk, repeat from * to end. (32 sts)
Bind off.

Finishing:
Felt and block the knitted material, then form into a square bowl shape as in the photograph.

A
TEXTURED
VASE
COVER

Think soft sculpture in this long slipcover for a glass or metal cylinder. Ringed with ribs and two rows of embossed leaves, the cover elevates a simple vase to a conversation piece.

Skill Level: ◖■■▭

Materials

Yarn: Berroco Ultra Alpaca 215yd (198m)/3.5oz (100g) ball

Color: 6202

Amount: 1 ball

Total Yardage: 215yd (198m)

Needles: 1 set US 8 (5mm) double-pointed needles or size to get gauge

1 crochet hook US size H (5mm) or size to match needles

1 cable needle US 8 (5mm) or size to get gauge

Gauge: 20 sts and 26 rows = 4" (10cm) in pattern stitch

Finished Size: 9½" (24cm) in circumference and 9" (24cm) tall (unstretched)

Note: The final vase cover is designed to stretch around a cylinder approx 11" (27.9cm) in circumference.

INSTRUCTIONS

Using a crochet hook, chain 8 sts. Pull the loop through the 1st chain to make a ring. Put the loop on a knitting needle and pick up 7 additional sts on four double-pointed needles.

Round 1: K in back and front of each st. (16sts)

Round 2: K even.

Round 3: *K 1, M1, k. 1, rep from * to end (24 sts)

Round 4: K even.

Round 5: *K1, M1, k k2, rep from * to end (32 sts)

Round 6: K even.

Round 7: *K1, M1, k3, rep from * to end. (40sts)

Round 8: K even.

Round 9: *K1, M1, k4, rep from * to end. (48sts)

Round10: K even.

Round 11: *P5, k1, rep from * to end.

Repeat previous row 10 times.

Begin the embossed leaves:

Round 1: *P3, p2 tog, M1R, k1, M1L, p2 tog, p3, k1, rep from * to end.

Round 2: *P4, k3, p4, k1, rep from * to end.

Round 3: *P3, k2 tog, yo, k1, yo, ssk, p3, k1, rep from * to end.

Round 4: *P3, k5, p3, k1, rep from * to end.

Round 5: *P2, k2tog, k1, yo, k1, yo, k1, ssk, p2, k1, rep from * to end.

Begin second tier of leaves:

Round 1: P5, k1, *p3, p2 tog, M1R, k1, M1L, p2 tog, p3, k1, rep from * ending p5, k1, p3, p2 tog, M1r, k1 to end.

Round 2: M1l, p2 tog, p3, k1, *p4, k3, p4, k1, rep from * ending p4, k2.

Round 3: K1, p4, k1, *p2, p2 tog, k1, yo, k1, yo, k1, p2 tog, p2, k1, rep from * ending p2, p2 tog, k1, yo, k1.

Round 4: Yo, k1, p2 tog, p2, *k1, p3,k5, p3, rep from, ending * k1, p3, k3.

Round 5: K2, p3, *k1, p1, p2 tog, k2, yo, k1, yo, k2, p2 tog, p1, rep from * ending k1, p1, p2 tog, k2, yo, k1.

Round 6: Yo, k2, p2 tog, p1,* k1, p2, k7, p2, rep from * ending k1, p2, k4.

Round 7: K3, p2, *k1, p2 tog, k3, yo, k1, yo, k3, p2 tog, rep from * ending k1, p2 tog, k3, yo, k1.

Round 8: Yo, k3, p2 tog, *k1, p1, k9, p1, rep from * ending k1, p1, k5.

Round 9: K4, p1, * k1, p1, put next st on cn and hold to front. P next st, k1 from cn, k5, put next st on cn and hold to back. K next st, p1 from cn, p1, rep from * ending k1, p1, put next st on cn and hold to front. P next st, k1 from cn, p1, k4.

Round 10: K2, *put next st on cn and hold to front, k next st, p1 from cn, p1, k7, p2, rep from * ending k1, p2, k4.

Round 11: K3, p2, * k1, p2, put next st on cn and hold to front, p next st, k1 from cn, k3, put next st on cn and hold to back, k next st, p1 from cn, p2, rep from * ending k1, p2, put next st on cn and hold to front, p next st, k1 from cn, k2.

Round 12: K1, put next st on cn and hold to back, k next st, p1 from cn, p2, *k1, p3, k5, p3, rep from * ending k1, p3, k3.

Round 13: K2, p3, *k1, p3, put next st on cn and hold to front, p next st, k1 from cn, k1, put next st on cn and hold to back, k next st, p 1 from cn, p3, rep from * ending k1, p3, put next st on cn

Round 6: *P2, k7, p2, k1, rep from * to end.
Round 7: *P1, k2 tog, k2, yo, k1, yo, k2, ssk, p1, k1, rep from * to end.

Round 8: *P1, k9, p1, k1, rep from * to end.
Round 9: *P1, put next st on cn and hold to front, p next st, k1 from cn, k5, put next st on cn and hold to back, k next st, p st from cn, p1, k1, rep from * to end.
Round 10: P2, k7, p2, k1, rep from * to end.

Round 11: *P2, put next st on cn and hold to front, p next st, k st from cn, k3, put next st on cn and hold to front, k next st, p st from cn, p2, rep from *to end.
Round 12: *P3, k5, p3, k1, rep from * to end.
Round 13: *P3, put next st on cn and hold to front, p next st, k1 from cn, k1, put next st on cn and hold to back, k next st, p1 from cn, p3, k1, rep from * to end.
Round 14: *P4, k3, p4, k1, rep from * to end.
Round 15: *P5, k1, rep from * to end.
Repeat previous round 16 times.

and hold to front, p next st, k1, k1.

Round 14: Put next st on cn and hold in back, k next st, p1 from cn, p3, *k1, p4, k3, p4, rep from * ending k1, p4, k2.

Round 15: K1, p4, k1, *p5, k1, rep from * to end.

Round 16: *P5, k1, rep from * to end.

Repeat Round 16 twice more.

Bind off.

This pattern can be altered to cover cylinders of other dimensions. Use the gauge as a guide for figuring the necessary number of stitches and rows. To keep the pattern symmetrical, stitches must be added in increments of 8, or about 1⅝" (4cm) in width, with the new stitches distributed evenly among the 8 segments of the pattern. The ribbed "stems" may be made shorter or taller, depending on the height of your cylinder.

Key to Leaf Pattern Chart

l	Knit
–	Purl
O	Yarn over
∧	Purl together
ᴗ	Make 1, twisted to the right
ᴄ	Make 1, twisted to the left
⟋	Knit 2 together
⟍	SSK
⟋	Put st on cable needle and hold to front, purl next st, knit st from cn
⌐	Put next st on cable needle and hold to back, knit next st, purl st from cn

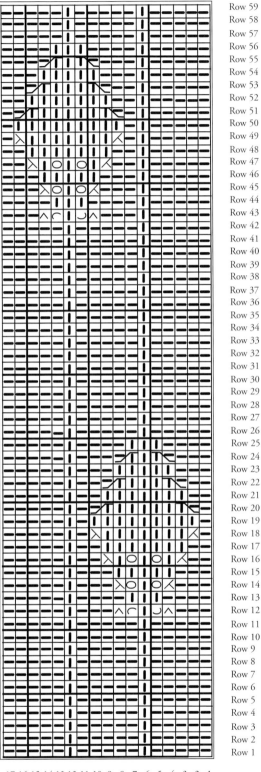

Row 59
Row 58
Row 57
Row 56
Row 55
Row 54
Row 53
Row 52
Row 51
Row 50
Row 49
Row 48
Row 47
Row 46
Row 45
Row 44
Row 43
Row 42
Row 41
Row 40
Row 39
Row 38
Row 37
Row 36
Row 35
Row 34
Row 33
Row 32
Row 31
Row 30
Row 29
Row 28
Row 27
Row 26
Row 25
Row 24
Row 23
Row 22
Row 21
Row 20
Row 19
Row 18
Row 17
Row 16
Row 15
Row 14
Row 13
Row 12
Row 11
Row 10
Row 9
Row 8
Row 7
Row 6
Row 5
Row 4
Row 3
Row 2
Row 1

17 16 15 14 13 12 11 10 9 8 7 6 5 4 3 2 1

A WRAP IN CHUNKY YARN

You won't want to let go of this divine throw made of the softest alpaca worked in a fluted rib pattern. Zig-zag borders at the top and bottom of the wrap echo the knit-and-purl triangles in the stitch pattern.

Skill Level: ■■■□

Materials

Yarn: Misti Alpaca Chunky 108yd (99 m)/3.5oz (100g) skein

Color: 3317

Amount: 7 skeins

Total Yardage: 648ye (594m)

Needles: US 13 (9mm) or size to get gauge
One crochet hook US M (9mm) or size to match needles

Gauge: 10.5 sts and 16 rows = 4" (10cm)

Finished Size: Approx. 20" (51cm) x 60" (153cm)

INSTRUCTIONS

Using waste yarn and a crochet hook, chain 110 sts.

Turn the chain face-down with bumps at back of chain upward. Using the project yarn pick up 53 sts, one in every other bump in rear of chain.

Note: All slipped stitches are slipped purlwise.

Rows 1, 2, and 3: Sl 1, k1 (for two-stitch selvage), p1, *k7, p1, repeat from * until 2 sts remain. K2.

Row 4: Sl 1, k1 (for two-stitch selvage), K2, *p5, k3, repeat from * ending with p5, k4 (includes two-stitch selvage).

Row 5: Sl 1, k1, p3, *k3, p5, repeat from * ending with k3, p3, k2.

Rows 6, 7, and 8: Sl 1, k1, k4, *p1, k7, repeat from * ending with p1, k4, k2.

Row 9: Repeat row 5.

Row 10: Repeat row 4.

Repeat rows 1 to 10 until the piece measures 60" (152.4cm).

Top border:

Row 1: Sl 1, k2, k2 tog twice, k3. Turn.

Row 2: SSK, k4, k2 tog. Turn.

Row 3: Sl 1, k5. Turn.

Row 4: SSK, k2, k2 tog. Turn.

Row 5: Sl 1, k3. Turn.

Row 6: SSK, k2 tog. Turn

Row 7: K2 tog.

Bind off.

Reattach yarn for next sawtooth point.

Row 1: K8, turn.

Left
A detail of the easy knit-and-purl pattern that creates pleats in the fabric of this chunky throw.

Opposite
The diamond shapes that form the nexus of the pattern are carried forward into points at each end of the chunky throw.

Work rows 2 to 7 as established above. Bind off. Working 8 stitches at a time, complete three more sawtooth points.

Work remaining 11 sts as follows:
Row 1: K3, k2 tog twice, k4. Turn.
Row 2: Ssk, k1, k2 tog three times. Turn.
Work rows 3 to 7 as established above. Bind off.

Finishing:
At the cast-on edge, unravel the waste yarn and pick up 53sts. Work the bottom border following the same instructions as for the top border.

Key to Pattern Chart

The chart shows the entire width of the throw. The green lines to the left and right sides of the chart mark the dividing lines between full pattern repeats in the middle, and the half pattern repeats at either end.

ꙅ   Slip1 purlwise without working stitch

•   Knit on right side and wrong side

| knit on right side, purl on wrong side

—   Purl on right side, knit on wrong side

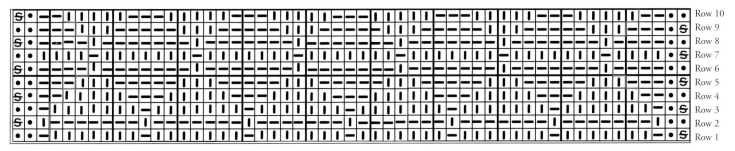

DINING KNITS

Knits for the dining room include cute egg hats to keep them warm, a table runner, placemats, a tea cosy, a felted bowl plus a felted vase cover and felted cocktail mats, and a bag tidy to hang on the back of the door.

A border of Irish moss stitch frames the slip-stitch pattern in the center. The metallic sheen of the silk yarn will add a touch of glamor to an intimate late-night supper table, where delicate china and glassware will shine out against its lustre. Note this is is a smaller-than-usual placemat, designed for small supper dishes.

Skill Level: ◖■☐◗

Materials

Yarn: Jaeger Pure Silk DK
137yd (125m)/1.75oz (50g)

Color: 005 Slate

Amount: 1 ball per placemat

Total Yardage: 137yd (125m) per placemat

Needles: US 6 (4mm) or size to obtain gauge

Gauge: 23 sts and 30 rows = 4" stocking stitch

Finished Size: 14" [35.5cm] wide x 10" [25.5cm] deep

Special Abbreviation

KW = K1 wrapping yarn twice around needle.

INSTRUCTIONS

Cast on 64 stitches.

Make border as follows:

Row 1: K1, p1, repeat to end of row.
Row 2: K1, p1, repeat to end of row.
Row 3: P1, k1, repeat to end of row.
Row 4: P1, k1, repeat to end of row.

Repeat these 4 rows until 16 rows have been worked.

Work main part as follows:

Row 1: P1, k1 for 10sts, k4 *KW, k4, repeat from * to last 10sts, p1, k1 to end.
Row 2: P1, k1 for 10sts, p4 *slip 1, p4, repeat from * to last 10sts, p1, k1 to end.
Row 3: K1, p1 for 10sts, k4 *KW, k4, repeat from * to last 10sts, k1, p1 to end.
Row 4: K1, p1 for 10sts, p4 *slip 1, p4, repeat from * to last 10sts, k1, p1 to end.

Repeat these 4 rows until 48 rows have been worked.

Work top edge of border as follows:

Row 1: P1, k1, repeat to end of row.
Row 2: P1, k1, repeat to end of row.
Row 3: K1, p1, repeat to end of row.
Row 4: K1, p1, repeat to end of row.
Repeat these 4 rows until 16 rows have been worked.
Bind off.

Finishing:

Cover with a cotton tea towel and press very lightly according to instructions on yarn label.

Opposite
This is a small, elegant placemat designed for intimate late-night suppers for two, using nothing but the best silverware, naturally!

A Silken Placemat

A Black & White Runner

A dramatic chevron pattern in pure silk yarn will dress up a space for any occasion. The peaks and valleys of the pattern are created by balancing an equal number of increases and decreases.

Skill level ◧■▢▷

Materials

Yarn: Debbie Bliss Pure Silk 137yd (125m) 1.75oz (50g) per skein
For MC, Color 27001
For CC, Color 27003

Amount: 2 skeins MC, 1 ball CC

Total Yardage: 27yd (250m) for MC, 137yd (125m) for CC

Needles: US 6 (4mm) or size to get gauge

Gauge: 29½ sts and 30 rows = 4" (10cm) in pattern stitch

Finished Size: Approx. 12" (30.5cm) wide and 39" (99cm) long

Special abbreviations:

Sl 2 = Insert right needle in second stitch on left needle and slip two stitches knitwise
Sl m = slip marker
Pm = place marker
Rm = remove marker

INSTRUCTIONS

With MC, cast on 93 sts.

Row 1: With MC, k4, pm, ssk, k11, *sl 2, k1, p2sso, pm, k 11, repeat from * until 6 sts remain; ssk, pm, k4.

Row 2: Sl 1 purlwise (selvage st) k3, sl m, sl 1 wyif; *k5 , in next st k1, yo, k1 (two sts increased) k5, sl m, sl 1 wyif, repeat from * until 4 sts remain, sl m, k4.

Row 3: Sl 1, purlwise (selvage st), change from MC to CC, k3, sl m, ssk, k11, *sl 2, rm, k1, p2sso, pm, k 11, repeat from * until 6 sts remain. Ssk, sl m, k4.

Row 4: Sl 1 purlwise (selvage st), k3,* sl m, sl 1 wyif, p5, p1, yo, p1, p5 in next st, repeat from * until 5 sts remain, sl 1 wyif, sl m, k4.

Row 5: Change from CC to MC, sl 1purlwise (selvage st), k3, sl m, ssk, *k11, sl 2, sl m, k1, p2sso, repeat from * until 6 sts remain. Ssk, sl m, k4.

Row 6: Repeat row 2.

Repeat rows 3 to 6 until piece measures 7⅜" (18.5cm) from bottom points, ending with row 4 (CC stripe). Cut CC.

With MC, repeat rows 3 and 4 until piece measures 31⅝" (80.3cm) from bottom points.

Attach CC. Work rows 3 to 6 until piece measures 39" (99cm), ending with MC on row 6. **Next row:** using MC bind off while working row 3 of pattern stitch.

Bottom
Judicious placement of increases and decreases creates the zig-zag line of the chevron pattern, shown here in the black and white of the border.

Opposite
In a single color, the chevron pattern takes on a herringbone texture with strong vertical ribs. It steps into the background against its two-color cousin at each end of the table runner.

A Frilly Tea Cozy

Your favorite teapot will be dressed for company in this chic cozy, with its layers of flounces in black and white. The ruffles are knit separately and attached to a foundation piece, which has openings for the teapot's spout and handle.

Note: Circular needles are preferred for knitting back and forth to allow greater maneuverability in joining ruffles to foundation pieces.

INSTRUCTIONS

First foundation piece:
With Color A and a circular needle, cast on 44 sts.
Rows 1 to 5: Knit.
Row 6: K1, p until 1 st remains, k1.
Rows 7 and 9: Knit.
Row 8 and 10: Rep row 6. Break yarn. Set aside.

Make first ruffle:
With separate strand of A and another circular needle, cast on 88 sts.
Rows 1 and 2: Knit.
Row 3: (WS): Purl.
Row 4: (RS): Knit.
Rows 5 to 9: (WS): Work in St st.
Row 10: *K2 tog, repeat from * to end. (44 sts). Break yarn.

Skill level:	■■■□

Materials

Yarn:	Classic Elite Bazic Wool 65yd (59m)/1.75oz (50g) ball
Color:	For Color A, Color 2916 Natural For Color B, Color 2913 Black
Amount:	3 balls Color A, 2 balls Color B
Total Yardage:	195 yd (177m) for Color A, 130 yd (118m) for Color B
Needles:	Three US 9 (5.5mm) circular needles 16" (40.6cm) long, or size to get gauge One set US 9 (5.5mm) double-pointed needles, or size to get gauge
Gauge:	16.5 sts and 24.5 rows = 4" (10cm) in St st.
Finished Size:	Approx. 21" (53.3 cm) in circumference and 7" (17.8cm) tall. Fits a medium teapot.

Join ruffle to foundation piece:
Layer the ruffle on top of the foundation piece so that the wrong side of the ruffle lays against the right side of the foundation piece. Arrange the pieces so that first stitch of the ruffle lines up with first stitch of foundation piece, the second stitch of ruffle lines up with second stitch of foundation, and so on.

Using a new strand of A, and a third circular needle, k tog the first st on the ruffle and the first st on the foundation piece. In the same way, join each stitch of foundation piece and ruffle across the row. Turn work.
Continuing with A, k1, p until 1 st remains, k1.
Next row: Knit.
Repeat previous two rows twice more.

Next row: (WS): K1, p until 1 st remains, k1. Break yarn.

Next row: Join Color B and knit across.

Next row: K1, p until 1 st remains, k1. Break yarn and set aside.

Second ruffle:

With B, and a separate circular needle, cast on 88 sts and make another ruffle, as instructed above. Using B, join the black ruffle to the foundation piece, as above. Turn work.

Next row: (WS): Continuing with B, k1, p until 1 st remains, k1.

Next row: (RS): Knit.

Repeat the previous two rows once more.

Next row: (WS): K1, p until 1 st remains, k1. Break yarn.

Next row: With A, K5, k2tog, k9, k2tog, k8, k2 tog, k9, k2tog, k5. (40 sts)

Row 6: K1, p until 1 st remains, k1. Break yarn and set aside.

Third ruffle:

With A, and separate circular needle, cast on 88 sts and make another ruffle, as instructed above. With A, join the ruffle to the foundation piece, as above, and set aside. Break yarn.

At this point, the foundation piece should have 27 rows, not counting the rows on the attached ruffles. Join two sections of foundation

Note: Change from circular to double-pointed needles as necessary

Round 28: (RS): *With A, work across one piece of tea cozy as follows: k4, k2tog, k8, k2tog, k8, k2tog, k8, k2tog, k4 (36sts). Pick up second piece and rep from * to end. (72 sts).

Round 29: Knit even.

Round 30: K7, k2tog, rep from * to end. (64 sts)

Round 31: Knit even.

Round 32: K3, k2tog, *k6, k2tog, rep from * to last 3 sts, k3. (56 sts)

Round 33: Knit even.

Round 34: *K 5, k2 tog, rep from * to end. (48 sts) Break yarn.

Round 35: With B, knit even. Set aside.

Fourth ruffle:

Using a separate strand of Color B and another circular needle, cast on 96 sts. Join as before.

Round 1: Knit.

Round 2: Purl.

Rounds 3 to 9: Knit.

Round 10: *K 2tog, repeat from * to end. Join the ruffle to the foundation as instructed above.

Continue with the foundation:

Round 36: K2, k2tog, *k4, k2tog, rep from * ending k2. (40 sts)

Round 37: Knit.

Round 38: *K3, k2tog, repeat from * to end. (32sts)

Round 39: Knit.

Round 40: *K2, k2tog, rep from * to end. (24 sts)

Round 41: Knit. Break off B. Pick up A.

Round 42: *K1, k2tog, rep from * to end. (16 sts)

Round 43: Knit.

Round 44: *K tog, rep from * to end. (8 sts)

Round 45: Repeat previous row. (4 sts)

Run the yarn twice through live sts and fasten off, or keep 4 sts on needles and make a loop.

To make a loop, * bring the yarn across the back of the work, without turning it, k 4.

Repeat from * until the the cord measures approx. 2" (5cm) or twice the desired length of the finished loop.

Sl 2, k2 tog, p2sso.

Fasten off, leaving a tail to secure the end of the cord into the loop.

Finishing:

Join the two sides of the foundation at the bottom with seams approx. 1½" (3cm) long, leaving openings for the spout and the handle. Block.

Above left and right

Your teapot is dressed for the occasion. The construction of the tea cozy leaves both the handle and spout free for pouring, without the fuss of removing the tea cozy altogether.

BOWL ME OVER!

This shallow felted bowl is the perfect container for anything that strikes your fancy, from a collection of seashells to an arrangement of colorful citrus fruit. You could also keep it on the hall console table as a safe-keeping place for keys.

Skill level: ◼◼◼◻
Materials:

Yarn:	Lamb's Pride Worsted 190yd (173m)/4oz (113g)
Color:	For MC, Color M22 Autumn Harvest
	For CC, Color M110 Orange You Glad
Amount:	1 ball MC, 1 ball CC
Total Yardage:	190yd (173m) 4oz (113g) for MC, 190yd (173m)/4oz (13g) for CC
Needles:	One set US 13 (9mm) double-pointed needles or size to get gauge
	Crochet hook US M (9mm) or size to match needles
Gauge:	Approx. 10 sts and 12 rows = 4" (10cm) before felting
	Approx. 12.5 sts and 18.5 rows = 4" (10cm) after felting
Finished Size:	Approx. 6" (15.25cm) in diameter and 2" (5cm) deep

INSTRUCTIONS

With a crochet hook and the MC, chain 8 sts, then pull the loop through the first chain to make a ring. Put the loop on a knitting needle and pick up 7 additional sts on four dp needles.

Round 1: K in back and front of each st. (16 sts)
Round 2: K even
Round 3: *K1 M1, k1, rep from * to end. (24 sts)
Round 4: K even.
Round 5: *K1, M1, k2, rep from * to end. (32 sts)
Round 6: K even.
Round 7: *K1, M1, k3, rep from * to end. (40 sts)
Round 8: K even.
Round 9: *K1, M1, k4, rep from * to end. (48 sts)
Round10: K even.
Round 11: *K1, M1, k5, rep from * to end. (56 sts)
Round 12: K even.
Round 13: *K1, M1, k6, rep from * to end. (64 sts)
Round 14: K even.
Round 15: Change from MC to CC. *K1, M1, k7, rep from * to end. (72 sts)
Rounds 16 and 17: K even with CC.
Round 18: K even with MC.
Rounds 19 and 20: K even with CC.
Rounds 21 and 22: K even with MC.
Next two rounds: Change from MC to CC,

*k2tog, k7, rep from * to end.
Change from CC to MC. Work 1 round even.
Bind off.

Finishing:
Felt and block into shape.

Above and opposite
This shallow felted bowl in orange will
make you smile. It is knit in the round
from the bottom up, with subtle changes
of color on the sides.

A Felted Vase Cover

A subtle fawn cover makes a design statement all its own. Knitted in the round, from the bottom up, the cover hides flower stems and adds texture to a tableau.

Skill level: ■ ■ ■ ☐

Materials:

Yarn:	Berroco Ultra Alpaca 215 yd (192m)/3.5oz (100g) skein
Color:	6202
Amount:	1 skein
Total yardage:	215 yd (192m)/3.5oz (100g) skein
Needles:	One set US 10 (6mm) double-pointed needles, or size to get gauge One crochet hook US J (6mm) or size to match needles
Gauge:	19.5 sts and 33 rows = 4" (10cm) after felting
Finished Size:	Fits a cylinder 11" (2.5cm) in circumference and 9" (22.5cm) tall

INSTRUCTIONS

With a crochet hook, chain 8 sts, pull the loop through the first chain to make a ring. Put the loop on a knitting needle and pick up 7 additional sts on four double-pointed needles.

Round 1: K in back and front of each st. (16sts)
Round 2: K even.
Round 3: *K 1, M1, k1, rep from * to end (24 sts)
Round 4: K even.
Round 5: *K1, M1, k k2, rep from * to end (32)
Round 6: K even.
Round 7: *K1, M1, k3, rep from * to end 40)
Round 8: K even.
Round 9: *K1, M1, k4, rep from * to end. (48sts)
Round10: K even.
Round 11: *K1, M1, k7, rep from * to end. (54 sts)
Knit even for 73 rounds [approx. 12½"(32.5cm)]

Bind off.

Finishing:
Felt and block around the vase.

Note: This pattern can be altered to cover cylinders of other dimensions. Use the felted gauge as a guide for figuring the necessary number of stitches and rows. Count on 5 stitches for each inch (2.5cm) in width and 8 rows for each inch (2.5cm) in height.

Fun egg cozies add warmth and style to breakfast. These egg "hats" are designed to keep the eggs warm, and are quick to knit and felt. A touch of embroidery adds a contemporary touch.

Skill Level: ◼◼◻◻

Materials:

Yarn:	Plymouth Galway worsted 210yd (192 m)/3.5oz (100g) ball
Color:	For Color A, Color 135 (hot pink), for Color B, Color 152 (chocolate brown)
Amount:	1 ball MC, 1 ball CC
Total yardage:	210yd (192 m) for Color A, 210 yd (192m) for Color B DMC embroidery floss, 1 skein each Color 938 (chocolate brown) and Color 604 (hot pink)
Needles:	One set US 11 (8mm) double-pointed needles or size to get gauge
Gauge:	13 sts and 16.5 rows = 4" (10cm) before felting 16½ sts and 31 rows = 4" (10cm) after felting.
Finished Size:	Approx. 2¼" (5.7cm) in diameter at base and 3¼" (8.25 cm) tall.

Opposite page and above

Egg cozies add a dash of humor as well as style to breakfast time. The little hats are worked in the round on big needles, felted, and embellished with contrasting embroidery floss.

INSTRUCTIONS

Cast on 28 sts and distribute evenly among three or four double-pointed needles. Join.
Knit 6 rounds even.

Round 7: *K7, k2tog, repeat from * twice more, k1 (25 sts)
Rounds 8, 9, 10: Knit.
Round 11: K3, k2tog, *k6, k2tog, repeat from * once more, k4 (22 sts)
Rounds 12, 13, 14, and 15: Knit.
Round 16: K1, *k2 tog, k3, repeat from * three times more, k1. (18 sts)
Round 17: Knit.
Round 18: *K2tog, k1, repeat from * to end. (12 sts)
Round 19: Knit.
Round 20: *K2tog, repeat from * to end. (6 sts)

Run yarn through live sts twice. Fasten off.
Felt.

Finishing:
Using a tapestry needle and the full thickness of embroidery floss in the selected colors, stitch a series of diagonal lines about ¾" (2cm) high around each of the cozies. Place the bottoms of the lines about ¾" (2cm) above the rim of each egg cozy for design consistency.

COLORFUL HAT TRICKS

A Crossed-Stitch
Place Mat

Crossed stitches in varying colors create a rich woven pattern in this table mat designed for your dining table, with yarn made of bamboo giving these placemats a subtle sheen. While the stitch pattern is demanding, the results are irresistible. This makes a perfect gift for a friend.

Skill level:	◼◼◼◻
Materials:	
Yarn:	Classic Elite Bam Boo 77yd (70m)/1.75oz (50g)
Color:	For Color A, 4904 Antilles Aqua For Color B, 4991 Aqua Print
Amount:	3 balls Color A and 2½ balls Color B for each placemat.
Total Yardage:	231yd (210m) for Color A, 193yd (175m) for Color B
Needles:	US 6 (4mm) and US 9 (5.5mm) or sizes to get gauge 1 crochet hook size G (4mm) or size to match needles 1 US 6 (4mm) cable needle or size to match needles
Gauge:	36 sts and 25 rows = 4" (10cm)
Finished Size:	Approx. 18½" (46.25cm) by 12½" (31.25cm)

Note: The instructions for crossing stitches in this pattern make use of a cable needle, although the work goes faster without one. Try the alternate method for crossed stitches, see the illustrations for basketweave stitch on page 19.

INSTRUCTIONS

With smaller needles and Color A, cast on 147 sts.
Knit 1 row.
Change from smaller to larger needles and begin pattern st. (multiple of 3)

Row 1: (RS) With B, k2, * place next st on cn and hold to front, k2, move st from cn to r needle without working it, rep from * ending k1.

Row 2: (WS) With A, *p2, sl 1 wyif, repeat from * to last 3 sts, p3.

Row 3: With A, k1 * sl first 2 sts on l needle to r needle, put next st on cn and hold to front, slip first two sts on r needle back to l needle, transfer st from cn to r needle without working it, k2, rep from * to last 2 sts, k2.

Row 4: With B, p3, *sl 1 wyif, p2, repeat from * to end.

Repeat rows 1-4 until piece measures 12½" (31.25cm) ending with row 1.

Bind off row: (WS): *P3tog, place st on r needle back on l needle, repeat from * to end. Fasten off.

Finishing:
With crochet hook and Color A, work 1 row slip stitch around perimeter of placemat. Press lightly.

TIP

To help keep sides even, draw yarn taut when changing colors. Be sure as well to knit the first two stitches of each row very tightly, on the tips of the needles, to compensate for any looseness in last stitch on previous row.

Work slip stitch border tautly, going down a size in the crochet hook if necessary, to prevent edges from curling.

Above and opposite page
This basketweave pattern results from crossed stitches
on right-side rows. Worked in solid and variegated
strands of bamboo yarn, it creates a thick fabric that is
perfect for your table. The slip-stitch crochet border
keeps the edges tidy.

A COCKTAIL COASTER SET

Brighten up the cocktail hour with these easy-to-make felted coasters in tropical colors. A six-pack will make a thoughtful hostess or holiday gift.

Skill level: ◼☐☐▷

Materials:

Yarn:	Plymouth Galway worsted 210yd (192m)/3.5oz (100g) ball
Colors:	136, 145, 146, 147, 154, and 156
Amount:	1 ball each color
Total Yardage:	210yd (192 m) for each color
Needles:	US 11 (8mm) or size to get gauge
Gauge:	16½ sts and 31 rows = 4" (10cm) after felting in stockinette stitch
Finished Size:	Approx. 4" (10cm) by 4" (10cm)

INSTRUCTIONS

Make six, one in each color.

Cast on 19 sts.

Rows 1, 2, and 3: Knit.
Row 4: K2, p15, k2.
Row 5: Knit.
Repeat rows 4 and 5 until there are 25 rows of St st, ending with RS row.
Next 2 rows: Knit
Next row: Bind off.

Felt and block to shape. Add cocktails!

A CABLE BAG TIDY

Simply, a clever way to keep those plastic bags at bay. This tidy knits up

quick and is decorated with a jaunty cable rope pattern.

Special Abbreviations:

C4B = cable 4 back. Slip next 2 stitches onto a cable needle and leave at the back of the work, k2, then k2 from the cable needle.

C4F = cable 4 front. Slip next 2 stitches onto a cable needle and leave at the front of the work, k2, then k2 from the cable needle.

T4B = twist 4 front. Slip next 2 stitches onto a cable needle and leave at the back of the work, k2, then p2 from the cable needle.

T4F = twist 4 front. Slip next 2 stitches onto a cable needle and leave at the front of the work, p2, then k2 from the cable needle.

INSTRUCTIONS

With No 8 needles, cast on 46 sts.

Work 9 rows of k2, p2 rib.

Knit 2 rows.

Next row: P15, place marker, p16, place marker, p15.

Place cable pattern as follows:

RS: Knit to 1st marker, work 16 sts of cable pattern, knit to end of row.

WS: Purl to 1st marker, work cable pattern, purl to end of row.

Cable pattern:

Note: Work rows 1 and 2 for the first time only.

Row 1: (RS) P2, k4, p4, k4, p2.

Row 2: K2, p4, k4, p4, k2.

Row 3: P2, C4F, p4, C4B, p2.

Row 4: K2, p4, k4, p4, k2.

Row 5: P2, k2, T4F, T4B, k2, p2.

Row 6: K2, p2, k2, p4, k2, p2, k2.

Row 7: P2, k2, p2, C4F, p2, k2, p2.

Row 8: K2, p2, k2, p4, k2, p2, k2.

Row 9: P2, k2, T4B, T4F, k2, p2.

Skill level:	■■■□
Materials:	
Yarn:	Rowan Cotton Rope 63yd (58m)/1.75oz (50g)
Color:	064 Calypso
Amount:	3 balls
Total Yardage:	189yd (173m)
Needles:	US 8 (5mm) or size to obtain gauge 1 pair US 8 (5mm) dpns
Other Materials:	2 stitch markers, cable needle, 40" (1m) thin elastic (optional)
Gauge:	15 sts and 20 rows = 4" (10cm) stockinette stitch
Finished Size:	5" (12.5cm) wide x 18½" (46cm) deep

Row 10: K2, p4, k4, p4, k2.

Repeat cable pattern from Row 3 seven times or until cable pattern measures 15½" (36cm) ending on row 10.

Next row: (RS: knit to marker) P2, C4B, p4, C4F, p2.

Purl next 3 rows. Remove markers.

Beginning on RS, work 9 rows of k2, p2 rib.

Bind off.

Hanging cord:

Using two dpns, cast on 4 sts and make 6" (15cm) of I-cord. Bind off.

Finishing:

Fold lengthwise and using mattress stitch, join side seam. Fold cord in half and attach to the top of the side seam. Thread elastic through the purl bumps on the WS of the ribbing at the bottom.

BEDROOM KNITS

Comfort is the key word in the bedroom zone. The projects include a fabulous cable bed cushion cover, a bolster cover, a throw, and a dressing table mat in relaxing colors.

A HOT WATER BOTTLE COVER

Super-soft yarn makes this hot water bottle cover a comfort next to your skin. Its stylish cable stands out against a background of reverse stockinette stitch.

Skill Level: ■■■▢
Materials
Yarn: Rowan Classic Yarns Cashsoft DK 142yd (130m)/1.75oz (50g)
Color: 507 Savannah
Amount: 2 balls
Total Yardage: 284yd (260m)
Needles: US 7 (4.5mm) or size to get gauge
Gauge: 20 sts and 32 rows = 4" (10cm) in reverse St st
Finished Size: To fit a 2-quart hot water bottle measuring approx 7½" (19cm) wide and 13" (33cm) tall

INSTRUCTIONS

Cast on 70 sts, including 2 selvage sts.
Row 1: (RS): P29, k12, p29.
Row 2: (WS): K16, M1, k2, M1, k11, p12, k11, M1, k2, M1, k16. (74 sts)
Row 3: P31, k4, C8F, p31.
Row 4: K17, M1, k2, M1, k12, p12, k12, M1, k2, M1, k16. (78 sts)
Row 5: P33, k12, p33.
Row 6: K18, M1, k2, M1, k13, p12, k 13, M1, k2, M1, k18. (82 sts)
Row 7: P35, C8F, k4, p35.
Row 8: K19, M1, k2, M1, k14, p12, k14, M1, k2, M1, k19. (86 sts)
Row 9: P 37, k12, p37.
Row 10: K20, M1, k2, M1, k15, p12, k15, M1, k2 M1, k20. (90 sts)
Row 11: P39, k4, C8F, p39.
Row 12: K39, p12, k39.
Row 13: P39, k12, p39.
Row 14: Repeat row 12.
Row 15: P39, C8F, k4, P39.
Row 16: K repeat row 12.
Row 17: P39, k12, p39.
Row 18: K39, p12, k19.
Row 19: P39, k4, C8F, p39.
Rep rows 12 to 19, working even, until piece measures 4" (10cm), ending with WS row.

Establish facing for zipper:
Next row: (RS): Bind off 1 st, k2 selvage sts, work remainder of row in pattern, as established.
Next row: (WS): Bind off 1 st, work remainder of row in pattern, as established. (88sts)
Next row: K2, work remainder of row in pattern, as established, until 2 sts remain, k2.

Work even in pattern stitch, with garter stitch selvage at each end of work, until piece measures 9½" (24cm) in length, ending with a RS row.
Next row: (WS): K18, ssk, pm, k2, pm, k2tog,

Above
The cable that is the focal point of the hot water bottle cover runs all the way to the top of the neck. The cover closes with a zipper in the back (not shown).

k14, p12, k14, ssk, k2, k2tog, k18. (84 sts)
Next row: (RS): Maintaining selvage, work in pattern until 2 sts before marker, p2tog, p2, sl m, p2tog tbl, work in pattern until 2 sts before next marker, p2tog, p2, sl m, p2tog tbl, work to end. (80 sts)
Next row: (WS): Work in pattern until 2 sts before marker, ssk, k2, k2tog, work in pattern until 2 sts before next marker, ssk, k2, k2tog, work in pattern until end. (76 sts)

Repeat right side and wrong side decrease rows until 9 rows have been completed and 36 sts have been decreased. (52 sts remain)

Work even, maintaining selvage and cable pattern, until neck measures approx. 3" (7.5cm) long. Bind off.

Finishing:
Block. Sew the bottom seam. Sew the back seam to the bottom of the zipper. Insert the zipper *(see page 22 for instructions)*.

Right and above
A neat line of increases embedded in stockinette stitch follows the curve of the hot water bottle which is encased in the cover. The bottom front (shown) and back (not shown) of the cover are sewn together.

TIP

To prevent sagging purl loops on the cable pattern, always knit the first stitch of the C8F tightly as it is 'jumping' across 4 other stitches. Similarly, knit the first stitch off the cable needle tightly as well.

A BOLSTER WITH BOBBLES

Skill level

Skill level ◼◼◼▢

Materials

Yarn:	ALLHEMP6 150yd (137m) 3.2 oz (90g)
Color:	For MC, Pearl For CC, Classic Hemp
Amount:	2 skeins MC, 1 skein CC
Total Yardage:	300yd (274m) for MC, 150 yd (137m) for CC
Needles:	US 5 (3.75mm) circular needle 24" (61cm) long, or size to get gauge
Gauge:	20 sts and 27 rows = 4"(10cm) in bobble pattern stitch
Finished Size:	To fit bolster pillow 15" (38cm) long and 19" (48.25cm) in circumference

A cascade of bobbles spills over a bolster pillow covered in hemp. The cover is knit back and forth in one piece and closes with a row of bobble buttons and buttonholes.

Notes:

A circular needle is recommended for back-and-forth knitting to give greater flexibility in accommodating increases and decreases on sides of pillow cover.

It will be easier to get gauge if the hemp is washed before it is used. To prevent tangles, insert skeins in an old pair of panty hose before putting them in the washer. Air dry.

Special instructions:

MB (Make Bobble): In next st, *k1,p1, rep from * twice more total 6 sts). Turn.

*K6, turn, p6, rep from * once more, turn, k6, turn, sl 3 purlwise, k3 tog, p3sso. (1 st remains)

Carry CC in back of work, catching it with MC in the stitch immediately before and after each bobble.

INSTRUCTIONS

Cast on 6 sts. (includes 2 selvage sts.)

Row 1: K1, inc 1 st in each of next four sts, k1. (10 sts)

Row 2: P1, inc. 1 st in each of next 8 sts, p.1 (18 sts)

Row 3: K1, *inc. 1 in nest st, k1, rep from * until 1 st remains, k1. (26 sts)

Row 4 and all even rows through to row 22: Purl.

Row 5: K3, k in back and front of the next st, 4, (one selvage stitch, plus 3, increasing in the third st), inc. 1, *k3, inc. 1, rep from * until 1 st remains, k1. (34 sts)

Row 7: K2, *inc. 1, k4, rep from * to end. (42 sts)

Row 9: *K5, inc. 1, rep from * until 2 sts remain, k2. (50 sts)

Bobble Row 1:

Row 11: K2, inc. 1, k6, inc. 1, k1, attach Color B, MB. Drop color B, pick up Color A, k3, inc. 1, k4, inc. 1, k1, MB, k5, inc.1, k4, MB(sts 35), k1, inc. 1, k6, inc. 1, k1, MB, k4, inc. 1, k5, MB, k2. (58 sts)

Row 13: K5, inc. 1, *k7, inc. 1, rep from * until 4 sts remain. K4 (66 sts)

Row 15: *K8, inc. 1, rep from * until 2 sts remain. K2. (74 sts)

Row 17: K2, inc. 1, *k9, inc. 1, rep from * until 9 sts remain. K9. (82 sts)

Row 19: K6, inc. 1, *k10, inc. 1, rep from * until 6 sts remain. K6 (90 sts)

Row 21: K12, inc.1, * k11, inc. 1, rep from * until 1 st remains. K1 (98 sts)

Row 22: Purl to end.

Row 23: Cast on 7 sts to create placket for buttons. Knit.

Row 24: Bind off 1 st, k2, p until 2 sts remain, k2.

Maintaining garter stitch selvage on each end, work 2 rows St st.

Bobble Row 2:

Next row: RS. K 11, MB in next st, *k15, MB in next st, rep from * 4 times more. K to end.

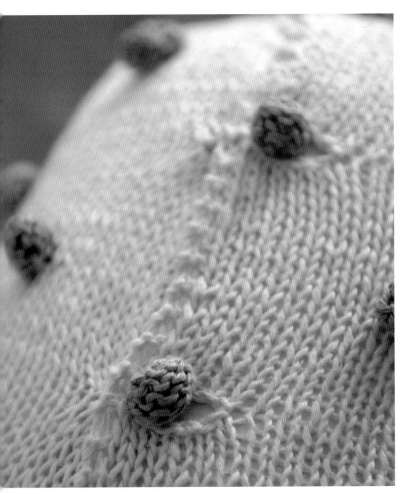

Maintaining two-stitch garter stitch selvage at each end, work in St st for 9 rows, ending with WS row.

Bobble Row 3:

K 4, mark last st knit with scrap yarn for bobble button (to be attached later), *K 15, MB in next st, rep from * 4 times more, work until 7 sts remain in row. Work 1-row buttonhole. K to end. Maintaining two-stitch garter stitch selvage at each end, work in St st for 9 rows, ending with WS row.

Rep. from Bobble Row 2 until there are a total of 10 bobble rows along length of pillow; 5 of Bobble Row 2 and 5 of Bobble Row 3.

Work 2 rows St st.

Next Row (WS): CO 1 st for seam allowance. P until 2 sts remain, k2.

Decrease for side of pillow:

Row 1: Bind off 7 sts of button placket, k11, * k2 tog, k10, repeat from * until 1 st remains. K 1. (90 sts)

Row 2 and all even-numbered rows through **Row 20:** Purl.

Row 3: K6, *k2 tog, k9, rep from * until 5 sts remain, k5. (82 sts)

Row 5: K2, *k2 tog, k8, rep from * until 8 sts remain. K 8. (74 sts)

Row 7: *K7, k2tog, rep from * until 2 sts remain. K2. (66 sts)

Bobble Row 4:

Row 9: k4, k2tog, k5, k2tog, MB, *k4, k2 tog, k4, k2tog, MB, rep from * three times more. K2.

Row 11: K1, *k2tog, k5, rep from * until 6 sts remain. K6 (50 sts)

Row 13: *K4, k2tog, rep from * until 2 sts remain. K 2. (42 sts)

Row 15: K1, *k2tog, k3, rep from * until 4 sts remain. K4. (34 sts)

Row 17: K3, *k2tog, k2, rep from * to end.

(26 sts)

Row 19: K1, *k2tog, k1, rep from * until 2 sts
remain. K2. (18 sts)

Row 21: K1, *k2tog, rep from * until 1 st
remains. K1 (10 sts.)

Row 22: P1, *p2tog, rep from * until 1 st
remains. P1 (6 sts)

Run yarn twice through remaining loops and
fasten off.

Bobble buttons:
Make 5

Cast on 1 st. Work the bobble as above. Fasten off
the end st, leaving a long tail. Thread the tail onto
a tapestry needle and weave it in an out of the
edges of the bobble around the perimeter. Stuff
the bobble with bits of matching yarn and draw
its tail closed. Fasten off. Sew the bobble to the
pillow cover.

Finishing:

Sew the side seams. Tack down the corners of the
button placket.

Above
Rows of bobbles in reverse
stockinette stitch and a contrasting
color liven up an otherwise plain
cover for a small bolster pillow.

Opposite
A row of bobble buttons secures the
pillow cover on the bolster. The
bobble buttons are stuffed with bits
of matching yarn to firm them up.

A CABLE CUSHION

The classic technique of cable is brought right up to date

with this stylish cushion cover which would make a fashion

statement on either a traditional or contemporary sofa.

Skill level: ■■■□

Materials:

Yarn:	Jaeger Roma 137yd (125m)/1.75oz (50g)
Color:	018
Amount:	3 balls
Total Yardage:	411yd (375m)
Needles:	US 6 (4mm) or size to obtain gauge
Gauge:	18 sts and 28 rows = 4" (10cm) stockinette stitch 28 sts and 32 rows = 4" (10cm) in cable pattern
Finished Size:	12" (30.5cm) square

Special Abbreviations:

T6F = TWIST 6 FRONT: Slip next 3 sts onto cable needle and hold at front of work, purl next 3 sts from left-hand needle, then knit sts from cable needle.

T6B = TWIST 6 BACK: Slip next 3 sts onto cable needle and hold at back of work, knit next 3 sts from left-hand needle, then purl sts from cable needle.

INSTRUCTIONS

Front:

Cast on 84 sts.

Row 1: *P6, k3, p12, k3, p6, k6, rep from * once more. P 12.

Row 2: K 12, *p6, k6, p3, k12, p3, k6, rep from * once more.

Rows 3 and 4: Repeat rows 1 and 2.

Row 5: P6, *T6F, p6, T6B, p3, T6B, T6F, p 3, rep from * once more. P 6.

Row 6: K9, * p3, k6, rep from * until 9 sts remain. K9.

Row 7: P9, *T6F, T6B, p3, T6B, p6, T6F, p3, rep from * once more. P 3.

Row 8: K6,* p3, k12, p3, k6, p6, k6, rep from * once more. K6.

Row 9: P12, *k6, p6, k3, p12, k3, p6, rep from * once more.

Row 10: K6, *p3, k12, p3, k6, p6, k6, rep from * once more. K 6.

Rows 11 and 12: Repeat rows 9 and 10.

Row 13: P9, *T6B, T6F, p3, T6F, p6, T6B, p3, rep from * once more. P3.

Row 14: K9, *p3, k6, repeat from * until 3 sts remain. K3.

Row 15: P6, *T6B, p6, T6F, p3, T6F, T6B, p3, rep from * once more. P6.

Row 16: K12, *p6, k6, p3, k12, p3, k6, rep from * once more.

These 16 rows are the pattern.

Repeat pattern 3 more times or until work measures 12" (30.5cm) from cast on edge. Bind off. Block the front before starting to knit the back.

Back, Lower Panel:
Cast on 53 stitches.
Work stockinette stitch until work measures 7" (17.75cm) from cast on edge.
Next row: *K1, p1, repeat from * to end of row. Repeat this row until 10 rows of seed stitch have been worked.
Bind off.

Back, Upper Panel:
Cast on 53 stitches.

Work stockinette stitch until work measures 3½" (8.25cm) from cast on edge.
Next row: *K1, p1, repeat from * to end of row. Repeat this row until 10 rows of seed stitch have been worked. Bind off.

Finishing:
Lay the back panels with RS down and seed stitch bands overlapping.
Lay the front with RS up on top of the back panels. Join all four seams using mattress stitch, making sure that the seed stitch bands are joined together at the edge.

Optional: Place three Velcro spots evenly across the overlapping rib stitch bands. Sew in place.

Opposite page
Neat stitching joins the back and front of this
cable pillow cover, ensuring a professional finish.

Above left
Bands of seed stitch mark the overlapping edges
on the back of the pillow cover, providing a
decorative edge on the opening for a pillow
form.

Above right
Undulating cords of stockinette stitch join
and separate and join again in cables that
run up and down the front of a stylish
pillow cover against a background of
reverse stockinette stitch.

A CABLE CUSHION **89**

DRESS UP A TABLE

Color changes streak a circular dressing table mat which uses short rows to achieve the maximum effect. The mat is knit in wedges that form a circle, with the first and last rows being grafted together. The pointed edges create a chic effect.

Skill Level:	◀■■■▢
Materials:	
Yarn:	Fiesta Rayon Boucle 240yd (219 m)/ 4oz (113g) skein
Color:	2136 Coyote
Amount:	1 skein
Total Yardage:	240yd (219 m)/ 4oz (113g) skein
Needles:	US 6 (4mm) or size to get gauge
Gauge:	Approx. 20 sts and 40 rows = 4" (10cm) in garter st.
Finished Size:	Approx. 12" (30.5cm) in diameter

INSTRUCTIONS

Using waste yarn and a crochet hook, chain 52 sts.

Turn the chain face-down with bumps at back of chain upward. Using the project yarn, pick up 24 sts in every other bump in the chain.

Row 1: (WS): Sl 1, pm, k19, yo, k2 tog, yo, k2 tog. Turn.

Row 2: With work in the left hand, and using knit-on or cable method, cast on 5 sts. K6, yo, p2 tog, yo, k2 tog, k17, sl 1, rm, bring yarn forward between needles, sl first st on right needle back to left needle. Turn.

Row 3: Sl 1, pm, k17, yo, k2 tog, yo, k2 tog, k5.

Note: One stitch is slipped and wrapped at the end of each even-numbered row, and a second stitch is slipped and wrapped at the beginning of each odd-numbered row, beginning with row 2, and ending with row 19 of the pattern. On the final row, each slipped stitch and its wrap are picked up and knit.

Row 4: Ssk, k4, yo, p2 tog, yo, k2 tog, k15, sl 1, rm, bring yarn forward between needles, sl first st on right needle back to left needle. Turn.

Row 5: Sl 1, pm, k15, yo, k2 tog, yo, k2 tog, k4.
Row 6: Ssk, k3, yo, p2 tog, yo k2 tog, k13, sl 1, rm, bring yarn forward between needles, sl first st on right needle back to left needle. Turn.

Row 7: Sl 1, pm, k13, yo, k2 tog, yo, k2 tog, k3.
Row 8: Ssk, k2, yo, p2 tog, yo, k2 tog, k11, sl 1, rm, bring yarn forward between needles, sl first st on right needle back to left needle. Turn.

Row 9: Sl 1, pm, k11, yo, k2 tog, yo, k2 tog, k2.
Row 10: Ssk, k1, yo, p2 tog, yo, k2 tog, k9, sl 1, rm, bring yarn forward between needles, sl first st on right needle back to left needle. Turn.

Row 11: Sl 1, pm, k9, yo, k2 tog, yo , k2 tog, k1.
Row 12: Ssk, yo, p2 tog, yo, k2 tog, k7, sl 1, rm, bring yarn forward between needles, sl first st on right needle back to left needle. Turn.

Row 13: Sl 1, pm, k7, yo, k2 tog, yo, k2 tog. Turn.

Row 14: With work in the left hand, and using knit-on or cable method, cast on 5 sts, k6, yo, p2 tog, yo, k2 tog, k5, sl 1, rm, bring yarn forward between needles, sl first st on right needle back to left needle. Turn.

Row 15: Sl 1, pm, k5, yo, k2 tog, yo, k2 tog, k5.
Row 16: Ssk, k4, yo, p2 tog, yo, k2 tog, k 3, sl 1, rm, bring yarn forward between needles, sl first st on right needle back to left needle. Turn.

Row 17: Sl 1, pm, k3, yo, k2 tog, yo k2 tog, k4.
Row 18: Ssk, k3, yo, p2 tog, yo, k2 tog, k1, sl 1, rm, bring yarn forward between needles, sl first st on right needle back to left needle. Turn.

Row 19: Sl 1, pm, k1, yo , k2 tog, yo k2 tog, k3.
Row 20: Ssk, k2, yo, p2 tog, yo, k2 tog, turn.

Row 21: Yo, k2 tog, yo, k2 tog, k2.
Row 22: Ssk, k1, yo, p2 tog, turn.

Row 23: Sl 1, yo, k2 tog, k1.
Row 24: Ssk, yo , p2 tog, yo, k2 tog, rm *k next
st along with wrap, repeat from * until 1 st
remains. K1.
Repeat rows 1 to 24 until a circle is formed.
Graft the ends together, including the yarn
overs in the stitch count.

Opposite
The dressing table cloth looks like a starburst,
radiating outward from the center toward
a sawtooth edging.

Above
At the center of the cloth there is a hole
that is a design element in itself.

A FURRY COVER

Using snuggly Jaeger Fur, this hot water bottle cover in black and white soft yarn is just begging to be hugged!

Note: Most of the pattern is in reverse stockinette stitch (rss) because the yarn is furrier on the purl side. For a neater color change, the first row of a new color is knit on the right side. With each color change twist, not cut and join, the yarn not in use with the active yarn in every other row.

INSTRUCTIONS

Front:
Using A and No 15 needles, cast on 16 sts.
Starting on a purl row, work 2 rows of rss.
Cont. with rss, cast on 2 sts at beg of next 2 rows.
Join in B. K next 2 rows, inc. 1 st at beg and end of each row.

Twist A with B, but continue to use B. Work even rss for 2 rows.
Change to A, cast on 5sts, k 2 rows.
Cast on 2sts, work even rss for 2 rows, twisting B with A at beg of first row.
Change to B, k 2 rows.
With B work even rss for 2 rows.
Change to A, k 2 rows.
With A work even rss for 2 rows.
Change to B, k 2 rows.
With B work even rss for 2 rows.
Change to A, bind off 2 sts, k 2 rows.
Bind off 5 sts, work even for 2 rows.
Change to B, k 2 rows.
With B work even with rss for 2 rows, dec. 1 st at beg and end of each row.

Skill level:	◧ ■ ■ ▢	
Materials:		
Yarn:	Jaeger Fur 22yd (20m)/ 1.75oz (50g) Jaeger Extra Fine Merino Aran 95yd (87m)/ 1.75oz (50g)	
Color:	Color A, 053 Jaguar, Color B, 048 Polar, Color C, 548 Black	
Amount:	For A, B, 3 balls. For C, 1 ball	
Total Yardage:	66yd (60m) for A, B; 95yd (87m) for C	
Needles:	US 15 (10mm) and US 7 (4.5mm) or sizes to get gauge	
Other Materials:	3 buttons ⅞" (2.3cm) diameter	
Gauge:	8 sts and 9 rows = 4" (10cm) in rss (Fur) 19 sts and 25 rows = 4" (10cm) seed stitch (Merino Aran)	
Finished Size:	10" [25cm] wide x 16" [40cm]	

Change to A, k 2 rows.
Bind off 2 sts at beg of each row.
With A work even rss for 2 rows. Bind off.

Back Lower Panel:
Using B and No 15 needles, cast on 11 sts.
Starting on a purl row, work 3 rows of rss.
Cont. with rss, cast on 2 sts at beg of next row.
Join in A. K to last st, inc. 1.
Next row: inc 1, k to end of row.
Twist B with A, but cont. to use A. Work even rss for 2 rows.
Change to B, work 20 rows rss changing color every 4 rows.
Note: Begin first row of new color with a k row.
Change to A, knit 2 rows.
With A, p to last st, dec 1.
Next row: Dec 1, k to end of row.
Change to B, knit 1 row.
With B, bind off 2 sts at beg of next row.
Work even rss for 2 rows. Bind off.
Work bottom band as follows:
With No. 7 needles and C, pick up 49 sts along the straight right-hand
edge of the panel (approx. 7 sts per stripe).

*K1, p1, repeat from * to end of row.
Repeat this row 9 times more. Bind off.

Back Upper Panel:
Using B and No 15 needles, cast on 3 sts.
Starting on a purl row, work 2 rows of rss.
Cont. with rss, cast on 2 sts at beg of next row.
With B, knit 1 row.
Join in A. Inc 1, k to end of row.
Next row: K to last st, inc 1.
Twist B with A, but cont. to use A. Work even rss for 2 rows.
Change to B, cast on 5sts. Knit 2 rows.
Cast on 2sts, work even rss for 2 rows.
Change to A, knit 2 rows.
With A, work even rss for 2 rows.
Change to B, bind off 2 sts, knit 2 rows.
Bind off 5 sts, work even for 2 rows.
Change to A, knit 2 rows.
Inc 1, k to end of row.
Next row: K to last st, inc 1.
Change to B, knit 2 rows.
Bind off 2 sts at beg of next row. Work even rss for 2 rows. Bind off.

Work buttonhole band as follows:
With No 7 needles and C, pick up 49 sts along the straight left-hand edge of the panel.
*K1, p1, repeat from * to end of row.
Repeat row 3 times more.
Next row: Work even k1, p1 for 10 sts, *bind off 4 sts, work even for 9 sts, repeat from * to last st, k1.
Next row: Work even k1, p1, for 10 sts, *turn, cast on 3 sts, sl 1 st right to left needle, yf, sl 1 st from left to right needle, yb, cast on 1 st, turn, work even for 9 sts, rep from * to last st, k1.
Work even k1, p1 for 4 rows. Bind off.

Finishing:
Lay back panels with RS down and button band on top of buttonhole band. Lay front, with RS up, on top of back panels. Join all the way round using mattress stitch, making sure button bands are joined at each edge. Sew on buttons.

A HIP PILLOW COVER

A spot of novelty yarn on a pillow designed for fun will banish the doldrums from any room. Fast and easy knitting will make this pillow the focal point in a modern setting. Teens will covet this cover.

Skill level: ◼◼◻◻

Materials:

Yarn:	Plymouth Hip 88 yd (80.5m)/ 1.75oz (50g) ball
Color:	1812
Amount:	5 balls
Total Yardage:	440yd (402.5m)
Needles:	US 9 (5.5mm), or size to get gauge
Gauge:	17 sts and 24 rows = 4" (10cm) in garter stitch
Finished Size:	Approx. 12" (30.5cm) by 16" (40.5cm)

Note: To make the seam lines more visible, create guides as you knit. On the second and last rows of each piece, pass contrasting waste yarn to the back and front between stitches, alternating with every stitch. Similarly, move the contrasting waste yarn alternately to the back and front on each row between the first and second stitches and between the next-to-last and last stitches.

INSTRUCTIONS

Pillow front:
With Hip yarn and size 9 needles, cast on 70 sts. (includes 2 selvage sts). Work in garter stitch, knitting every row, until the pillow is about 12" (30.5cm) long. Work 1 more row. Bind off.

Pillow back:
Make 2
Dimensions: Approx 10" (25.5cm) by 12" (30.5cm)
Cast on 44 sts. Work in garter stitch until the piece is the same length as the pillow front.

Finishing:
Sew the front of the pillow to the pillow backs, overlapping the back pieces at the center to create a vertical opening for a pillow form.

Opposite:
The novelty yarn used for this pillow cover makes its own statement, both in texture and in color.

A Tassel Tie-Back

A novelty yarn with both sheen and texture makes an oversized tassel that

adds a unique finishing statement to your décor. Use it as a curtain

tie-back, or attach a large cupboard key.

Skill level: ■■□□

Materials:

Yarn: Plymouth Margarita 88yd (80m)/1.75oz (50g) ball.

Color: 3422

Amount: 1 ball

Total Yardage: 88yd (80m)

Needles: US 9 (5.5mm) or size to get gauge
1 styrofoam ball 2" (5cm) in diameter

Gauge: Approx. 20 sts and 32 rows = 4" (10cm) in garter stitch

Finished Size: Approx. 7" (17.75cm) long

INSTRUCTIONS

Cast on 4 sts.

Row 1: K in back and front of each st. (8 sts)

Row 2: K even.

Row 3: Knit in back and front of each st. (16 sts)

Row 4: Knit even.

Row 5: *Knit in front and back of stitch, k1, rep from * to end. (24 sts)

Row 6: Knit even.

Row 7: K2, k in front and back of next st,* k3, k in back and front of next st, * end, k1. (30 sts)

Knit even until piece is approx 3" (7.6cm) long and will stretch around the styrofoam ball.

Make fringe:

*With work in the left hand, and using the knitted or cable cast-on method, cast on 30 sts. Bind off 31 sts.

With work in left hand, cast on 30 sts. Bind off 32 sts.

Rep from * until all sts are bound off. (20 lengths of fringe inches created.)

Finishing:

Wrap tassel around 2" (5 cm) styrofoam ball. Sew a seam, edge to edge, so that it lies flat against the ball. Wrap the yarn several times around the bottom of the ball. Tie off the yarn and hide the ends. To hang from a knob, cut a length of ribbon yarn about 12" (25cm) long. Attach one end to the knitting top of the tassel. Make a large loop (about 3½" (7cm)long) and attach the other end of the ribbon yarn to the top of the tassel. Hide the tails by running them inside the knitting.

To make I-cord to wrap around bottom of ball:

Use a circular needle or two double-pointed needles. With scrap yarn, cast on 3 sts. Pick up project yarn and knit 1 row. *Without turning, move the work from the left side to the right side of the circular needle. Tug the yarn across the back and knit 3 sts. Rep from * until the I-cord is long enough to fit around bottom of ball, approx. 2½" (6.5cm). Then wrap the I-cord around the bottom of the ball and graft the ends together.

You can protect your precious jewels when traveling with this beautiful silk-lined handknitted pouch.

Skill Level: ◖◼◼◼◻
Materials
Yarn: Debbie Bliss Pure Silk DK 37yd (33m)/1.75oz (50g)
Color: 05 Moss Green
Amount: 1 skein
Total yardage: 37yd (33m)
Needles: US 5 (3.75mm) or size to obtain gauge
Other Materials: 24" (60cm) satin ribbon ⅛" (0.3cm) wide
4½" wide x 12½" long (10cm x 33.5cm) satin lining fabric
Gauge: 26 sts and 32 rows = 4" (10cm) stockinette stitch
Finished Size: 4" (10cm) wide x 6" (15.25cm) high

Note: The lower edging is worked as a ribbon, not horizontally across the piece.

INSTRUCTIONS

Lower edging:
Cast on 5 sts.
Row 1: Sl1, k1, (yo twice), k2tog, k1.
Row 2: Sl1, k2, p1, k2.
Row 3: Sl1, k3, (yo twice), k2.
Row 4: Sl1, k2, p1, k4.
Row 5: Sl1, k1, (yo twice), k2tog, k4.
Row 6: Sl1, k5, p1, k2.
Row 7: Sl1, k8.
Row 8: Bind off 4 sts, k4.
Repeat rows 1 to 8 four times more.
Work rows 1 to 7 only.
Next row: Bind off 8 sts.

Front:
With remaining st on needle, pick up 25 sts along the straight edge of the piece just knitted.
Next row: Cast on 1 st, purl to end of row.
Starting with a knit row, work 4 rows of St st.

Diamond pattern:
Row 1: K4, *p1, k5, rep from * to last 5 sts, p1, k4.
Row 2: *P3, k1, p1, k1, rep from * to last 3 sts, p3.
Row 3: *K2, p1, k3, p1, k1, p1, rep from * to last 2 sts, k2.
Row 4: P1, *k1, p5, rep from * to last 2 sts, k1, p1.
Row 5: K2, *p1, k3, p1, k1, rep from * to last st, k1.
Row 6: *P3, k1, p1, k1, rep from * to last 3 sts, p3.
Repeat rows 1 to 6.
Row 13: K4, *p1, k5, rep from * to last 5 sts, p1, k4.

A Jewelry Pouch

Next row: Purl.

Work even St st until piece measures 4" (10cm) from pick up edge ending on a WS row.

Eyelet row:

K4, yo, k2tog, rep from * to last 3 sts, k3.
Next row: Purl.
Work even St st for 4 rows.

Work picot point bind off:

Bind off 2 sts, *pass st from right-hand needle to left-hand needle, cast on 2 sts, bind off 4 sts, rep from * to end of row. Cut yarn and fasten off.

Back:

With WS of work facing and starting with a slip knot on right-hand needle, pick up 25 sts along pick up edge.

Next row: Purl.

Starting with a knit row, work even St st until piece measures 4" (10cm) from pick up edge ending on a WS row.

Eyelet row:

K4, yo, k2tog, rep from * to last 3 sts, k3.
Next row: Purl.
Work even St st for 4 rowss.

Work picot point bind off:

Bind off 2sts, *pass st from right-hand needle to left-hand needle, cast on 2 sts, bind off 4 sts, rep from * to end of row. Cut yarn and fasten off.

Finishing:

Weave in the yarn ends. Lay the piece flat and use it as a template for the lining. Cut 2 pieces of

lining, each measuring approx. 4½" (11.4cm) wide by 12½" (33cm). Sew together the side seams of knitted bag. Fold the lining RS together, then sew the sides with a ¼" (.06cm) seam. Fold the top of the lining bag over by ½" (1.25cm) to reveal the RS of fabric. Carefully place lining bag inside knitted bag and tack in place with sewing thread along the fold-over edge. Lightly press.

Cut the ribbon in half and thread one piece through all the eyelets, beginning at one side seam. Thread the other piece through the eyelets beginning at other side seam. Knot the ends of each piece together to form the drawstring.

Above
The jewelry pouch ends in a delicate picot edging. Eyelets in the knitting make room for a drawstring of ribbon.

NURSERY KNITS

For the smaller members of the home, here is a soft and cuddly baby pillow cover, a beautiful baby blanket, and an heirloom Christmas decoration.

A WISE BLANKET

Whimsical owls watch over the young from their perches in a sea of white. The cute owls are created with cables and bobbles, a wise move for this soft and cuddly blanket.

Skill level	◼◼◼◻
Materials	
Yarn:	Debbie Bliss Cashmerino DK 120 (110 m)/1.75oz (100g) ball
Color:	18012 Melon for Color A 18002 White for Color B
Amount:	6 balls for Color A, 7 balls for Color B
Total yardage:	720yd (660m) for Color A, 840yd (770m) for Color B
Needles:	US 6 (4mm) or size to get gauge
Gauge:	20 sts and 28 rows = 4"(10cm) in St st, after blocking
Finished Size:	Approx. 35" (87.5cm) by 39½" (99cm)

Special abbreviations:

C6F Put three sts on cn and hold to front, k3, k3 sts from cn.

C6B Put three sts on cn and hold to back, k3, k3 sts from cn.

INSTRUCTIONS

With A, cast on 175 sts.

Seed stitch border:

Row 1: *K1, p1, repeat from * to end.
Repeat this row until piece measure 2" (5 cm). (14 rows)

Background:

Row 1: (RS) Using A, work 10 sts in seed st, as established. Attach B, k155 sts. (10 sts remain.)

Attach separate strand of A. *P1, k1, repeat from * to end.

Row 2: With A, *k1, p1 repeat from * 4 times (10 sts worked). Drop A and pick up B, p155. Drop B and pick up A, *p1, k1, repeat from * 4 times. Turn.

Repeat rows 1 and 2 for 3" (7.5 cm), ending with WS row. (20 rows)

Insert embossed owls:

Row 1: (RS): With A, work 10 sts in seed st, as established; with B, k15; *attach separate strand of A, k20, attach separate strand of B, k15, repeat from * 3 times. With A, work 10 sts in seed stitch, beginning with p1, k1.

Row 2: With A, work 10 sts in seed st, beginning with k1, p1; with B, p15, *with A, k20, with B, p15, repeat from * three times. With A, work 10 sts in seed st, beginning with p1, k1.

Row 3: With A, work 10 sts in seed st; with B, k15; * with A, p20, with B, k15, repeat from * 3 times. With A, work 10 sts in seed stitch, beginning with p1, k1.

Row 4: With A, work 10 sts in seed st, beginning with k1, p1, with B, p15, *with A, k2, p5, inc.1, p6, inc. 1, p 5, k2, with B, p15, repeat from * three times. With A, work 10 sts in seed st, beginning with p1, k1.

Row 5: With A, work 10 sts in seed st, with B, k15; *with A, p2, k3, C6B, C6F, k3, p2, with B, k15, repeat from * 3 times. With A, work 10 sts in seed st.

Row 6: With A, work 10 sts in seed st, with B, p 15, *with A, k2, p18, k2, with B, p15, repeat from * three times. With A, work 10 sts in seed st.

Row 7: With A, work 10 sts seed st, with B, k15, *with A, p2, C6B, k6, C6F, p2, with B, k15, repeat from * three times. With A, work 10 sts seed st.

Row 8: With A, work 10 sts seed st, with B, p15, *with A, k2, p7, k1, p1, k1, p1, p7, k2, with B, p 15 repeat from * three times. With A, work 10 sts seed st.

Row 9: With A, work 10 sts seed st, with B, k15, * with A, p2, k7, p1, k1, p1, k1, k7, p2, with B, k15, repeat from * three times. With A, work 10 sts seed st.

Row 10: Repeat row 8.
Row 11: Repeat row 9.
Row 12: Repeat row 8.

Row 13: With A, work 10 sts seed st, with B, k15, *with A, p2, k18, p2, with B, k15, repeat from * three times. With A, work 10 sts seed st.
Row 14: With A, work 10 sts seed st, with B, p15, *with A, k2, p 18, k2, with B, p15, repeat from * three times. With B, work 10 sts seed st.

Row 15: Repeat row 13.
Row 16: Repeat row 14.

Row 17: With A, work 10 sts seed st, with B, k15, *with A, p2, k3, C6B, C6F, K3, p2, with B, k15, repeat from * three times. With A, work 10sts seed st.

Row 18: Repeat row 14.

Row 28
Row 27
Row 26
Row 25
Row 24
Row 23
Row 22
Row 21
Row 20
Row 19
Row 18
Row 17
Row 16
Row 15
Row 14
Row 13
Row 12
Row 11
Row 10
Row 9
Row 8
Row 7
Row 6
Row 5
Row 4
Row 3
Row 2
Row 1

24 23 22 21 20 19 18 17 16 15 14 13 12 11 10 9 8 7 6 5 4 3 2 1

Key to owl pattern chart

I knit on right side, purl on wrong side

– Purl on wrong side, knit on right side

/ ssk (on wrong side)

**** k2tog (on wrong side)

∧ Purl 2 together

B Make bobble

Increase 1 in the same stitch

C6F Put 3 sts on cn and hold to front, k3, k3 sts from cn

Put 3 sts on cn and hold to front, p3, k3 sts from cn

Put 3 sts on cn and hold to back, k3, p3 sts from cn

C6B Put 3 sts on cn and hold to back, k3, k3 sts from cn

Row 19: With A, work 10 sts in seed st; with B, k15, *with A, p2, C6B, k6, C6F, p2; with B, k15, repeat from * three times. With A, work 10sts seed st.

Row 20: With A, work 10 sts seed st; with B, p15, *with A, k2, P3, k4, p4, k4, p3, k2; with B, p15, repeat from * three times. With A, work 10 sts seed st.

Row 21: With A, work 10 sts in seed st; with B, k15, *with A, p2, K3, p2, pick up horizontal bar between st just knit and next st, and knit into the back, front and back of it (3 sts made), turn. K3. Turn. Sl 2, k1, p2sso. Put first loop on right needle back on left needle and p2tog, p1. K4, p2, pick up horizontal bar between st just knit and next st, and knit into the back, front and back of it (3 sts made), turn. K3. Turn. Sl 2, k1, p2sso. Put first loop on right needle back on left needle and p2 tog, p1, k3, p2. With B, k15, repeat from * three times. With A, work 10 sts seed st.

Row 22: Repeat row 20.

Row 23: With A, work 10 sts in seed st; with B k15; *with A, p2, k3, put 3 sts on cn and hold to back, k3, p3 from cn, put 3 sts on cn and hold to front, p3, k3 from cn, k3, p2. With B, k15, repeat from * three times. With A, work 10 sts seed st.

Row 24: With A, work 10 sts seed st; with B, p15; *with A, k2, p6, k6, p6, k2; with B, p15 repeat from * three times. With A, work 10 sts seed st.

Row 25: With A, work 10 sts seed st, with B k15, *with A, p2, put 3 sts on cn and hold to back, k3, p3 sts from cn, p6, put 3 sts on cn and hold to front, p3, k3 from cn, p2; with B, k15, repeat from * three times. With A, work 10 sts seed st.

Row 26: With A, work 10 sts seed st; with B p15;

*with A, k 6, ssk, k6, k2tog, k6; with B, p15 repeat from * three times. With A, work 10 sts seed st.

Row 27: With A, work 10 sts seed st; with B, k15; *with A, p20, with B, k15, repeat from * three times. With A, work 10 sts seed st.

Row 28: With A, work 10 sts seed st; with B, p 15; *with A, k20; with B, p15, repeat from * three times. With A, work 10 sts seed st.

Repeat 3" (7.5cm) lengths of background and repeat owl pattern until there are five rows of owls and six background segments, ending with a RS row. Drop B.

With A, work 10 sts seed st, k 155 sts, work remaining 10 sts in seed st.

Rows 2 to 14: Work in seed st.
Bind off.

Skill level ◖■■■▢

Materials

Yarn:	Filatura di Crosa Baby Lovely, 93yd (85m)/ 1.75oz (50g)
	Filatura di Crosa Baby Bon Bon, 99yd (90m)/1.75oz (100g) ball.
Color:	A, Lovely, Color 3
	B, Bon, Color 14.
Amount:	3 balls A, 1 ball B
Total yardage:	279yd (255m) for Color A, 99yd (90m) for Color B
Needles:	US 6 (4mm) or size to get gauge
Gauge:	24 sts and 32 rows = 4" (10cm) in pattern stitch, before blocking 19 sts and 28 rows = 4" (10cm) in St st, after blocking
Finished Size:	Approx. 12" x 12" (30.5cm x 30.5cm)

INSTRUCTIONS

Note: All slipped sts are slipped purlwise.

Pillow front:
With A cast on 73 sts.
To create selvage for zipper, knit two rows.

Begin pattern:
Row 1: (WS): Purl.
Row 2: (RS): K1 selvage st, k4, *sl 1, k2tog, psso, k7, rep from * until 8 sts remain. Sl 1, k2tog, psso, k4, k1 selvage st. (59 sts)
Row 3 and 5: Purl.
Row 4: K1 selvage st, k2, *k2tog, k1, sl 1, k1, psso, k3, rep from * until 5 sts remain. Sl 1, k1, psso, k2, k1 selvage st. (45 sts)
Row 6: Change from A to B. K1 selvage st, sl 3 sts, *(k1, p1, k1, p1, k1) in next st, sl 5 sts, rep from * until 4 sts remain. Sl 3 sts, k1 selvage st. (73sts)
Row 7: With B, k1 selvage st, yf, sl 3 sts, yb, *k5, yf, sl 5, yb, rep from * until 9 sts remain. K5, yf, sl 3, k1 selvage st.
Row 8: Change from B to A. Knit.
Row 9 and Row 11: Purl.
Row 10: K1 selvage st, sl 1, k1, psso, *k7, sl 1, k2tog, psso, rep from * until 3 sts remain. K2tog. k1 selvage st. (59 sts)
Row 12: K1 selvage st, k1, *sl 1, k1, psso, k3, k2tog, k1 rep from * until 1 st remains. K1 selvage st. (45 sts)
Row 13: Purl.

Row 14: Change from A to B. K1 selvage st, (k1, p1, k1) in next st, *sl 5 sts, (k1, p1, k1, p1, k1) in next st, rep from * until 7 sts remain. Sl 5 sts, (k1, p1, k1) in next st, k1 selvage st. (73 sts)
Row 15: K1 selvage st, k3, * yf, sl 5, yb, k5, repeat from * until 9 sts remain. Sl5, k3, k1 selvage st.
Row 16: Change from B to A. Knit.
Row 17: Purl.
Work Rows 2 to 17 six times.
Bind off.

Pillow back:
With A, cast on 60 sts (includes 2 selvage sts).
To create placket for zipper, knit 2 rows.
Maintaining selvage sts, work in St st until back of pillow matches length of front of pillow.
Bind off.

Finishing:
Block pieces. Install zipper and sew seams together. Press lightly.

A Baby Pillow with Bobbles

Add panache to the nursery with this adorable baby pillow.

Puff balls in lively colors provide the accent in a two-toned slip stitch pattern.

Baby will adore it!

A SNOWFLAKE ORNAMENT

This brilliant bauble, inspired by Victorian embroidery, is a perfect keepsake for a baby ... and is destined become an heirloom in your Christmas decoration collection. The family will love it!

Skill level:

Materials:

Yarn: Debbie Bliss Cathay 109yd (100m)/1.75oz (50g)

Color: MC: 12 Dark Purple; CC: 16 Pewter

Amount: 1 ball of each color

Total yardage: 54yd (50m)

Needles: US 5 (3.75mm) or size to get gauge

Other Materials: 24" (61cm) satin ribbon ¼" (0.6cm) wide
Craft ball approx. 2.5" (6.4cm) diameter

Gauge: 22 sts and 30 rows = 4" stockinette stitch

Finished Size: Ball-shaped decoration approx. 2½" (6.4cm) diameter

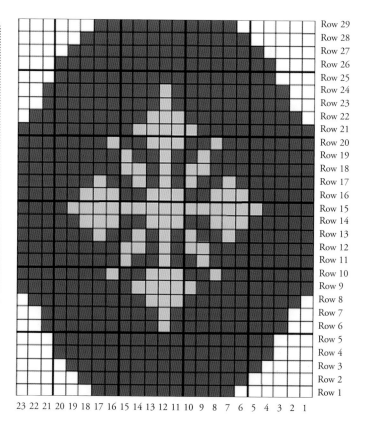

Rows 1–29 / Columns 23 22 21 20 19 18 17 16 15 14 13 12 11 10 9 8 7 6 5 4 3 2 1

INSTRUCTIONS
Make Two

Using MC, cast on 11 sts.
Work across chart using Fair Isle technique to strand unused Across back of work. Work in Stockinette stitch, knitting the odd rows and purling the even rows.

Finishing:
Press the knitted covers lightly. Gently stretch the covers around the craft ball. Using MC, join seams all the way around. Make sure that both covers are oriented in the same direction. Fold the ribbon in half. Join the ribbon at the halfway point to top of Christmas decoration. Tie the ribbon in an extravagant bow.

BATHROOM KNITS

Knit a bright yellow cotton bathmat, a snug-fitting wash glove,

and a buttercup-colored wash cloth for you or your guests.

Notes: This cotton yarn is laced with lycra. It stretches when it is knit and contracts once it is off the needles.

To create a guide line for seaming, weave a contrasting color yarn to the front and back of work on each row, between the first and second stitch and the next-to-last and last stitch. The guides will make it easier to sew a seam in this yarn, which has poor stitch definition.

INSTRUCTIONS

With CC, cast on 64 sts (including 2 selvage sts). Work 12 rows garter stitch.
*Drop CC, pick up MC, and work 10 rows garter stitch.
Drop MC, pick up CC, and work 2 rows garter stitch.
Rep from * until mitt measures 8" (20 cm) long. Maintaining stripe pattern, begin decreases.
Row 1: K2, k2tog, k25, ssk, k2, k2tog, k25, ssk, k2. (60 sts)
Row 2 and all even rows: Knit even.
Row 3: K2, k2tog, k23, ssk, k2, k2tog, k23, ssk, k2. (56 sts)
Row 5: K2, k2tog, k21, ssk, k2, k2tog, k 21, ssk, k2 (52 sts)
Row 7: K2, k2tog, k19, ssk, k2, k2tog, k19, ssk, k2 (48 sts)
Row 9: K2, k2tog, k17, ssk, k2, k2tog, k17, ssk, k2. (44 sts)

Row 11: K2, k2tog, k15, ssk, k2, k2tog, k15, ssk, k2 (40 sts)
Row 13: K2, k2tog, k13, ssk, k2, k2tog, k13, ssk, k2 (36 sts)
Row 15: Discontinue the stripe pattern, changing from MC to CC. K2, k2tog, k11, ssk, k2, k2tog, k11, ssk, k2. (32 sts)
Row 17: K2, k2tog, k 9, ssk, k2, k2tog, k 9, ssk, k2 (28 sts)
Row 19: K2, k2tog, k7 ssk, k2, k2tog, k7, ssk, k2. (24 sts)
Row 21: K2, k2tog, k5 ssk, k2, k2tog, k5, ssk, k2. (20 sts)
Row 22: Bind off.

Finishing:

Sew a seam along the side of the mitt. With a crochet hook and double strand of CC, make a chain 4" (10cm) long. Make a loop and secure it on the inside of the seam at the wrist.

Skill Level: ■ ■ □ □
Materials:
Yarn: Classic Elite Star 112yd (102.5m)/1.75 oz (50g) ball
Color: For MC, Color 5116, Natural For CC, Color 5101 Bleach
Amount: 2 balls MC, 1 ball CC
Total yardage: 224 (205m) for MC, 112yd (102.5m) for CC
Needles: US 8 (5mm) or size to get gauge Crochet hook US H (5mm) or same size as needles
Gauge: 23½ sts and 46 rows = 4" (10cm) in garter stitch, before washing; 25 sts and 55½ rows = 4" (10cm) in garter stitch, after washing
Finished Size: Approx 4¼" (11cm) in diameter and 9½" (24cm) in length

A STRIPED
BATH MITT

A stretchy cotton yarn is worked back and forth

in simple garter stitch creating subtle stripes for a bath mitt

that knits up quickly and easily. Treat yourself, or

make one for a friend.

So-Soft Washcloths

A reversible checked rib ripples across this desirable washcloth, which is worked in an Egyptian cotton. These quick and easy knits will add a finishing touch to a guest bath as well as to your ensuite.

Skill Level:	◼☐☐☐
Materials:	
Yarn:	Classic Elite Provence 205yd (186m)/3.5oz (100g)
Color:	2650 New Moon
Amount:	1 skein makes two washcloths
Total yardage:	205yd/186m
Needles:	US 5 (3.75mm) or size to get gauge
Gauge:	25.5 sts and 36 rows = 4" (10cm) in pattern st before washing and drying
	24 sts and 38 rows = 4" (10cm) in pattern st after washing and drying
Finished Size:	9" x 9" (23cm x 23cm) after washing and drying

INSTRUCTIONS

Cast on 55 sts.

Row 1: Sl 1, k2, *p1, k3, rep from * to end.
Row 2: Sl 1, *p1, k3, rep from * ending p1, k1.
Rows 3 and 5: Repeat row 1.
Rows 4 and 6: Repeat row 2.
Rows 7, 9, and 11: Repeat row 2.
Rows 8, 10, and 12: Repeat row 1.

Maintaining the slip-stitch selvage throughout, work pattern for a total of 86 rows [9½" (24cm)], binding off in pattern stitch on last row.

Finishing:
Wash and dry each washcloth.

A Quick Bath Mat

Treat yourself to the luxury of a thick and soft bath mat that works up quickly on large needles. Call it the big easy, a simple slip-stitch pattern adds depth to the fabric.

INSTRUCTIONS

Note: Use two strands of yarn throughout

To have cast-on edge match bind-off edge, use crochet cast-on as follows:
Chain 50 sts. Transfer loop from crochet hook to knitting needle. Turn over crochet chain so it faces right side down, with bumps showing from backs of chain loops. Draw loop of working yarn from back to front under each bump and put loop on knitting needle. Repeat until a total of 51 sts are on needle.

Establish borders
Row 1: (RS): Knit.
Row 2: Purl.
Row 3: K1, sl 1, k2, sl 1, pm, p until 5 sts remain, pm, sl 1, k2, sl 1, k1.
Row 4: K1, p1, k2, p1, sl m, k until 5 sts remain, sl m, p1, k2, p1, k1.
Row 5: Repeat row 4.
Row 6: Repeat row 3.

Begin pattern stitch, maintaining borders at sides:
Row 1: K1, sl 1, k2, sl 1, sl m, k4, inc. 1 in next st, k7; rep from * 4 times, k4, sl m, sl 1, k2, sl 1, k1. (56 sts)
Row 2: K1, p1, k2, p1, sl m,*k1, sl 1 purlwise wyib, rep form * until 2 sts remain before marker; k2, p1, k2, p1, k1.
Row 3: K1, sl 1, k2, sl 1, knit until 5 sts remain. Sl 1, k2, sl 1, k1.
Row 4: K1, p1, k2, p1, sl m,*k2, sl 1 purlwise wyib, rep form * until 1 sts remain before marker; k1, p1, k2, p1, k1.

Skill Level:	◼◼◼◻
Materials:	
Yarn:	Halcyon Yarn Casco Bay Bulky Chenille, 550 yd (503m)/1lb (454g) cone
Color:	110 Yellow
Amount:	2 cones
Total yardage:	1100yd (1006m)
Needles:	US 13 (9mm) One crochet hook US M (9mm)
Gauge:	Approx 11 sts and 20 rows = 4" (10cm) in pattern stitch, before washing and drying Approx. 12 sts and 21.5 rows = 4" (10cm) in pattern stitch, after washing and drying
Finished Size:	20" (51cm) x 28" (71cm)

Row 5: Repeat row 3.
Repeat rows 2-5 until piece measures approx 26½" (67cm), ending with even-numbered (WS) row.

Finish borders:
Row 1: (Decrease row) K1, sl 1, k2, sl 1, sl m, k6, *k2tog, k6, rep from * four times more, sl m, sl 1, k2, sl 1, k1.
Row 2: K1, p1, k2, p1, sl m, p until 5 sts remain; sl m, p1, k2, p1, k1.
Row 3: K1, sl 1, k2, sl 1, sl m, p until 5 sts remain; sl m, sl 1, k2, sl 1, k1.
Row 4: K1, p1, k2, p1, sl m, k until 5 sts remain; sl m, p1, k2, p1, k1.
Row 5: Knit across, removing markers.
Row 6: Purl across, removing markers.
Row 7: Bind off.

GLOSSARY OF TERMS

In this list you will find most of the terms you will come across when you are reading a pattern.

A Above markers: Knitting worked after markers were placed in certain stitches
As established: Continue to work in sequence or pattern as previously positioned, to keep the continuity of the design or pattern
As foll: Work the following instructions
As for back; as for front: Work piece identical to the one mentioned in the instructions
Asterisks: * * Used to designate the beginning and often the end of sequences that are to be repeated

B Back edge: Any edge on the back piece of an item

C Centimeter (cm): Metric unit of measurement that often appears along with inches in gauge schematic on yarn labels, garment schematics, or some direction measurements. One centimeter is about .4 inches; 1 inch is about 2.54 centimeters.

D Directions are for smallest size with larger sizes in parentheses: In instructions given for more than one size, the smallest size is listed first, with the progressively larger sizes grouped within parentheses
Do not turn work: Keep the work facing in the same direction as the row just completed

E Each side or each end: Work according to the directions both at the beginning and at the end of a particular row
Ending with RS row or end with WS row: The work is finished when you have completed a right side (RS) or wrong side (WS) row
Every other row: When increasing or decreasing, leave one row between shaping rows

F Fasten off: To secure the stitches at the end of a bound-off row, when only the last stitch remains. Cut the yarn and draw the cut end through the loop of this last stitch, pulling the end to tighten

G Gauge: Number of stitches and rows over one square inch, or a larger specified area of knitting, often a four-inch (10 centimetre) square

H Hold in back of work or hold in front of work: Applies to stitches on cable needle held in back or front of work as it faces you; found in cable patterns

I Inc (number of) sts evenly across row: Increase a specic number of stitches at even intervals across a row
In the same way or manner: Repeat the process previously described

K K the knit sts and p the purl sts: When a pattern has been established, work each stitch like the one below in the previous row as it faces you. A knit stitch on the right side looks like a purl stitch on the wrong side and vice versa. If the stitch now looks like a purl stitch on this row facing you, purl it (even though it was a knit stitch on the opposite side of the work).
Knitwise: Insert needle or work as if you were making a knit stitch

M Make one (M1): Increase one stitch by lifting the horizontal strand between two existing stitches onto the left needle to form a loop; knit the loop, twisting it, to make the added stitch
Make one left (M1L) Make 1, twisting the horizontal strand to the left in making the new loop
Make one right (M1R) Make 1, twisting the horizontal strand to the right in making the new loop
Multiple of (number) sts plus (number): The number of stitches required for working a pattern for one repeat (the multiple), and any extra stitches at the ends to frame the pattern or make it symmetrical

P Pattern repeat: The number of stitches needed to work a pattern once
Place marker(s) (pm): Place a marker on the

needle between stitches as a reminder to make an increase or decrease, indicate a pattern repeat, or some other change in the pattern

Place marker in work: Mark a specific row or stitch with a safety pin or yarn for shaping or measurement (for length of armholes, for example)

Preparation row: A row that sets up a pattern stitch but is not part of the actual pattern

Purlwise: Insert needle or work as if you were making a purl stitch

R **Remove marker(s) (rm):** Remove the marker(s) from the work

Rep between *'s: Repeat all the instructions from the first asterisk to the second one once more or as many times as indicated

Rep from *: Repeat all the instructions after the asterisk across the row or as many times as indicated, ending the rows as instructions say

Repeat from * around: Used when knitting with circular needles, this means to repeat the instructions after the asterisk until the end of the round, the point where the cast-on stitches were joined

Repeat from (numbered) row: Repeat previously worked instructions from the row with the designated number

Rep inc or rep dec: Repeat the increase or decrease as previously instructed

Rep (number) times more: Repeat the just-worked instructions as many times as designated

Reverse shaping: Used when pattern calls for two pieces that are mirror images of each other, as for right and left fronts

Right side: Refers to the right side of the finished garment when it is being worn [Right side of garment is not abbreviated as RS because it may be confused with RS of work below.]

Right side of work (RS): Refers to the outside of the garment, the part that shows when the garment is worn

Row 1 and all RS or odd-numbered rows: Used when all right-side rows, or all odd-numbered rows are worked the same way

Row 2 and all WS or even-numbered rows: Used when all wrong-side rows or all even-numbered rows are worked the same way

S **Same as:** Repeat the instructions given in another section of the pattern

Schematic: A scale drawing or diagram showing the measurements of all pieces of a project before it is assembled

Selvage st(s): An extra stitch (or stitches) at the sides of a piece used either to make a decorative edge or to making seaming easier

Slip markers (slm): Move markers from left needle to right when you come to them to keep each one in the same position row after row

Swatch: A sample of knitting made to test gauge or try out a pattern or colors

T **Through (number) row:** Work up to and including the row with the specified number.

Total length: The length of a finished garment from top to bottom

Turn or turning: Transfer(ring) your work from right hand to left hand after completing a row. The tip of each needle changes direction in this transfer and the opposite side of your work now faces you. The yarn is in position on the left needle tip to begin work.

W **Weave in ends:** On the WS, work tails into stitches so they do not unravel and do not show on the outside of the garment

With the right side (RS) facing: The side of the work that will face outside on the completed item now faces you for the specific procedure, such as when you pick up stitches

With the wrong side (WS) facing: The side of the work that will face inward on the completed garment now faces you

Work even: Continue working in pattern without increasing or decreasing

GLOSSARY OF TERMS continued

Work to correspond: Work one piece, or side of a symmetrical shape, so that it is a mirror image of the other side

Working yarn: Yarn being used to form new stitches and drawn from a ball, skein, or bobbin

Wrong side of work (WS): The side of the finished garment that faces inward when the garment is worn

SKILL LEVELS FOR KNITTING AS USED IN PROJECTS

Beginner ◖☐☐☐

Projects for first-time knitters using basic knit and purl stitches. Minimal shaping.

Easy ◖■☐☐

Projects using basic stitches, repetitive stitch patterns, simple color changes, and simple shaping and finishing.

Intermediate ◖■■☐

Projects with a variety of stitches, such as basic cables and lace, simple intarsia, double-pointed needles and knitting in the round needle techniques, mid-level shaping and finishing.

ABBREVIATIONS

[ ]	Work instructions within brackets as many times as indicated.
* *	Repeat instructions between asterisks as directed
*	Repeat instructions following the single asterisk as indicated.
alt	alternate, alternatexly
approx	approximately
beg	begin/beginning
bet	between
CC	contrasting color
cm	centimeter(s)
cn	cable needle
CO	cast on
cont	continue (ing)
dec	decrease, decreases, decreased, decreasing
dp	double-pointed needle(s)
foll	follow/follows/following
g	gram
inc	increase/increases/increasing
k	knit
k2tog	knit 2 stitches together
kwise	knitwise
lp(s)	loop(s)
m	meter
M1	make one stitch, an increase
M1L	make 1, twisting to the left
M1R	make 1, twisting to the right
MC	main color
mm	millimeter(s)
oz	ounce(s)
p	purl
pm	place marker
p2tog	purl 2 stitches together
Psso	pass slip stitch over
pwise	purlwise
rem	remain, remaining, remains.
Rev St st	reverse stockinette stitch
rm(s)	remove marker(s)

rnd(s)	round(s) in circular knitting
RS	right side
sc	single crochet
sk	skip
sl 1, k1, psso	slip one stitch knitwise, knit 1, pass slip stitch over the knit stitch
sl1, k2 tog, psso	slip one stitch knitwise, knit 2 together, pass slip stitch over the two stitches knitted together
sl2, k1, p2sso	slip 2 stitches knitwise, knit next stitch, pass two slipped stitches over the knitted stitch
sl 2, k2tog, p2sso	slip 2 stitches knitwise, knit 2 stitches together, pass 2 slipped stitches over the stitches that were knit together
sl	slip a stitch without working it
sl1k	slip 1 knitwise
sl1p	slip 1 purlwise
slm	slip marker
sl st	slip stitch
ssk	slip next two stitches knitwise individually from left to right needle, then insert tip of left needle through fronts of loops from right to left. Knit them.
st(s)	stitch or stitches
St st	stockinette stitch or stocking stitch
tbl	through the back loop
tog	together
WS	wrong side
wyib	with yarn in back
wyif	with yarn in front
yd(s)	yard(s)
yfwd	yarn forward
yo	yarn over
yon	yarn over needle

INDEX

ACKNOWLEDGMENTS

To Lynn, who more than anyone kept me in gear for this book, to Kate Buchanan, whose creativity rounded out the collection, Conny Jude for her great patience and attention to detail, Amanda Hancocks for her superb photography, and the knitters who test drove the patterns: Elaine Boyd, Beth Cundy, Judi Ladd, Ann McGarry, Paula Migliaccio, Deborah Peterson, Lindsay Woodel, and the knitting force of the Ocean State Knitting and Crochet Guild; Fina Cicerchia, Kristen Chambers, Valerie Deion, Cindy DiDonato, Susan DiNola, Gail Hatfield, Nuala McLaughlin, and Margaret Moone, and the guys who contributed more than they know, Larry, Jeff, and Michael.

Further thanks go to the manufacturers and distributors of the fine yarns used in this book:

Berroco at *www.berroco.com*

Brown Sheep Co. at *www.brownsheep.com*

Classic Elite Yarns at *www.classicelite.com*

Halcyon Yarn at *www.halcyonyarn.com*

Hemp for Knitting at *www.hempforknitting.com*

Jaeger yarns at *www.westminsterfibers.com*

Knitting Fever at *www.knittingfever.com*

Misti International at *www.MistiAlpaca.com*

Plymouth Yarn at *www.plymouthyarn.com*

Rowan Yarns at *www.knitrowan.com*

Tahki Stacy Charles at *www.tahkistacycharles.com*